'If it's
not
too much
trouble'

'If it's not too much trouble'

the challenge of the aged parent

Ann Benton

CHRISTIAN
FOCUS

ISBN 1-84550-302-3
ISBN 978-1-84550-302-4

© Ann Benton

10 9 8 7 6 5 4 3 2 1

Published in 2007
by
Christian Focus Publications,
Geanies House, Fearn, Ross-shire,
IV20 1TW, Scotland, UK

www.christianfocus.com

Cover design by Moose77.com

Printed by CPD Wales

CONTENTS

This book is dedicated
to the memory of
Charles Edward Benton
1917–2006
and also to
'Charlie's Angels': Monika Newcombe, Alison Parsons,
Carolyn Parsons, Linda Wade, Carole Walter

Thank you.

Prologue

I'm an old man:
get me out of here!

In which I describe how this whole issue raised its grey head.

The old man propped up on pillows is suddenly overcome by the all too familiar griping pains. He needs a bedpan and he needs it quickly. He presses his buzzer for a nurse but he is not optimistic. He presses it again and again with increasing urgency. He hangs on: no nurse. Tears roll down his cheeks as he feels the warm familiar softness oozing underneath him and the malodorous stench reaches his nostrils. The old man hangs his head in shame. He presses again and again. After ten minutes a nurse appears, with a what's-all-the-fuss-about expression; she makes her assessment, sighs, draws the curtains around the old man and scurries away, promising to be back. Three quarters of an hour passes before two nurses appear. They chatter to each other as they do what has to be done. He says he is very sorry. They tell him not to worry. But he does. They tell him it is all right. But it certainly is not from where he is sitting.

On the other side of the ward another old man stares disconsolately at the food which has been deposited on his table by a woman in an overall. The woman spoke no English which is possibly why she failed to comprehend that his fingers are not sufficiently strong or nimble to open the cellophane packet enclosing the rectangle of cheese, nor can they insert his drinking straw into the carton of orange juice. He hopes a kindly visitor will come to help him access his meal. But visitors are a rare sight in this ward. The old man is defeated. And hungry.

Across the town in a flat which estate agents would describe as spacious and commodious with views of the park and handy for public transport, a social services occupational therapist is making her assessment. She has just trained an elderly woman, her son and daughter-in-law in the use of the hoist, a contraption resembling goalposts which has been fitted over the double bed in the master bedroom. The goalposts support a removable sling into which an unlucky punter can be placed, raised and transferred from bed to commode and back. The training procedure is one she has delivered frequently; it is scripted for idiots and delivered at a pace for the intellectually challenged. The class of three have listened meekly and patiently. They have allowed themselves to be hoisted and to hoist to the unsmiling satisfaction of the OT. It is not rocket science but she wants these rank amateurs to realise just how highly skilled she is. So she gives her professional opinion of the flat which is soon to receive home an elderly man suffering from Parkinson's disease, peripheral neuropathy and a collection of other problems which emanate from time spent sixty years ago as a Japanese prisoner-of-war. Plus MRSA.

The OT spots the old man's walking frame.

'He won't be needing that,' she says.

This is not a diagnosis any of the three has heard from a hospital doctor. They are still reeling from that pronouncement, when the OT adds, 'And of course, this is a **** flat.' (The word actually used is described in the dictionary as vulgar, so I will spare the reader's eyes.)

I suppose it was the words and attitude of the occupational therapist that put fire in my belly. We had been visiting my father-in-law in hospital for eight months. We had seen him deteriorate and become intensely desperate and depressed. The scenes recorded above were common. He was no longer receiving any treatment and the hospital wanted to be rid of him. But he refused to go into residential care and my mother-in-law was equally determined to have him home. In theory, care in the community is supposed to be 'a good thing', 'the way forward'. In practice, getting the support my father-in-law needed presented a huge problem. We will never know how hard the hospital department concerned worked at it but after three ineffectual months they admitted they were stumped and were still with increasing pressure suggesting residential care, even on a temporary basis in order to free up the hospital bed.

My parents-in-law had lived the typical careful and unselfish lives of their generation. Throughout their working lives they had quietly and regularly saved for a rainy day. These modest savings prevented them from receiving state help for the care which my father-in-law needed. So social services, apart from making their rather snotty assessment of my mother-law's arrangements, had nothing to offer us, not even constructive support or advice. The agencies who supply carers to self-funding clients were unable to come up with the requisite two carers three times a day. In an area where housing is so expensive there are never enough people to do low-paid work. Meanwhile all my father-in-law could say to us was:

'Get me out of here, son.'

'I'm doing my best, Dad.'

'Do more than your best. Get me out of here.'

So we did. We sprang him. It was a long hard road convincing the very particular but not particularly encouraging discharge people at the hospital, that I would supply the lack of carers and take responsibility for Dad's care at home. They had found an agency which could supply one morning and one evening carer. I committed myself to assisting morning and evening and in the afternoon bringing along a friend to help me. They did not trust my amateur status or believe that I could have such willing friends. It did not tick their boxes. Hence the hoist training. Fair enough. But after all the phone calls and hassle with people at the hospital and social services, the one thing I knew I wanted to do was get Dad out of the hands of professional 'carers'. Bring on the Christians.

1

THE FAMILY BUSINESS

*In which I apportion responsibility for the care
and comfort of the elderly.*

Everybody thinks someone else should do it. When there
are headlines about the poverty, neglect or abuse of old
people, which is pretty much a weekly occurrence, people
blame the government or social services.

'He's in his nineties and he's not a well man!'

'She can't manage in her flat. Have you seen it?'

'The council should do something!'

Whose business is it, that kind of situation?

It is undoubtedly the business of governments to put in
place policies and allocate resources which tackle poverty
and protect the vulnerable. I don't know of a political party
who would deny that that is their aim. But there will always
be a shortfall, if not of money, then of love. 'Professional carer'
is almost a contradiction in terms. How can a system which
has to continually account for value for money, which has
to buy and sell time by the minute, thoroughly address the

needs of the elderly or of anyone else. They attempt to, by their interminable checks, counter-checks and assessments. They have their tick-boxes and their conferences on best practice. I am not knocking such things, but the very fact that they have so many checks and balances shows that they recognise just how impossible a task this is.

Don't we all know that best practice is best not only in high standards for example in hygiene and safety, but in terms of immeasurable things, old-fashioned things, like warm hearts, friendship, genuine personal interest, going the extra mile. Things that take time but can't be categorised in a tick-box, things money can't buy. I have met professional carers who really care, but they didn't learn it from their NVQs. They don't get paid more for it and of course if they did, they would be the first to say that money devalued this extra that they gave. It sounds illogical but we know what they mean. It is as the Beatles said, 'Money can't buy me love.' Perish the thought.

What a frail old person needs in a carer is someone who is younger and fitter than him, someone who goes back a long way with him and understands where he is coming from, someone who speaks his language and understands his sense of humour, someone who was here yesterday and will be here again tomorrow, someone to share a reciprocal relationship. Hello? Isn't that a person profile of a son or a daughter? Might there not be a reasonable and beautiful balance in this: that the one who tended you as an infant when you were vulnerable and in need of assistance to perform the acts necessary to life, should now, years down the line, receive from you that same assistance?

The journalist Tom Utley commented in a feature for *The Daily Telegraph* that Britain's old people would be much better cared for in Africa.

'There is, as we all know, a very much better way of looking after the elderly than simply shovelling money in the direction of strangers, in the hope that they will look after them.

I am thinking of the most effective social security system ever devised by man or nature. It is a system that still operates in most primitive societies, but one which is on the verge of collapse in modern Britain. I mean, of course, the family.

In almost every way, I would much rather live here than in a mud-hut village in Africa.

But I reckon that the very old in the Third World, looked after by their families in communities bustling with life, have a much better time of it than a great many British OAPs, sitting around in care homes stinking of urine, watching afternoon television and counting the days or weeks until that rare visit from their young.'

Daily Telegraph 31/3/2006

A. But have you met my Dad?

'Well aged parent,' said Wemmick, shaking hands with him in a jocose way, 'how am you?'

'All right, John, all right!' replied the old man.

'Here's Mr Pip, aged parent,' said Wemmick, 'and I wish you could hear his name. Nod away at him, Mr Pip; that's what he likes. Nod away at him, if you please, like winking!'

'This is a fine place of my son's, sir,' cried the old man, while I nodded as hard as I possibly could. 'This is a pretty pleasure ground, sir. This spot and these beautiful works upon it ought to be kept together by the Nation, after my son's time, for the people's enjoyment.'

'You're as proud of it as Punch; ain't you, Aged?' said Wemmick, contemplating the old man, with his hard face really softened; 'there's a nod for you,' giving him a tremendous one; 'there's another for you,' giving him a still

more tremendous one;' you like that, don't you? If you're not tired, Mr Pip – though I know it's tiring to strangers – will you tip him one more? You can't think how it pleases him.'
Extract from *Great Expectations* by Charles Dickens

We might all wish, that if we were to have an aged parent live with us, we might have one as cheerful, contented, grateful and biddable as Wemmick's. It happens in real life, I dare say, but not that often I fear. One might argue that the Aged's sweetness of temperament was due to the utmost tenderness and care which he received from his son, but lest we should think that to be the case, Charles Dickens gives us, within the same novel, a counter example in 'the Old Growler', the father of the dutiful and loving Clara Barley. The Old Growler roars and bangs the floor of his upstairs bedroom all day long, calling for drink.

The sad fact is that older does not always mean wiser. And it hardly ever means more winsome. I know that one must beware of stereotyping the elderly and that the point I am making here does not apply across the board but this I have observed: unattractive habits which seemed amusing in youth can become entrenched and more dominant in old age. Handling the increasing loss of faculties is a test to the most upbeat disposition. There can be an air of 'having let oneself go' about old people – a woman who made it her business in younger days to be able, in a miniskirt, to enter and leave a Triumph Spitfire with the utmost elegance, now sits blithely with her crimplene skirt stretched across her gaping knees, showing her knickers. He who once rebuked his children sharply for messy eating now has egg and gravy down his jumper and sees no need to change it. To witness such a decline in standards can be painful to a son or daughter. Even more tragically, there can be the experience of dealing with an old woman who is most definitely your mother and who looks like your mother, but who doesn't even recognise you. And there is a sense in which you don't recognise her either.

In the very first book of the Bible we have the very first embarrassing Dad. This same man is one of Scripture's superstars, one of the heroes of faith. Which goes to show that the best of us can have our bad days. One of Noah's worst days is recorded for our learning:

> Noah, a man of the soil, proceeded to plant a vineyard. When he drank some of its wine, he became drunk and lay uncovered inside his tent. Ham, the father of Canaan, saw his father's nakedness and told his two brothers outside (Gen. 9:20-22).

It is easy to imagine Ham's response to what he saw. It was probably a mixture of disgust and ridicule. Maura Murphy in her tale of a life of hard living and hard drinking in Ireland tells this story about her husband, John, in his old age.

> John would get so drunk one of the barmen would often deposit him outside the cottage on his way home. But he wasn't always chauffeured around Rhode. He would usually stagger the half-mile home grinning and singing the Petula Clark song 'Sailor' all the way.
>
> One time he was so ****** he fell in the ditch and lost his false teeth and glasses. My teenage grandsons, Carmel's sons Kieran and Jonathan, were visiting at that time. They carried their granddad into the sitting room and put a packet of frozen peas on his head, showing great concern. But they were dying laughing inside. Each time the giggles possessed them they rushed into the kitchen to laugh, as silently as they could. Then they'd go back into John all sombre and caring.
>
> Extract from *Don't wake me at Doyles* by Maura Murphy

Who of us in our teens would not have responded like those two lads? It is hard to respect our parents or grandparents when they behave in such a disreputable way, when they let themselves down. No doubt Ham, though no teenager at over 100 years old, would have said the same thing. It seems likely that Ham invited his brothers to view the disgusting scene of their parent, naked and inebriated, and to enjoy a laugh at their father's expense. What was wrong with that? Isn't it what Noah deserved?

Shem and Japheth, however, have a deeper idea of respect than their brother:

> But Shem and Japheth took a garment and laid it across their shoulders; then they walked in backwards and covered their father's nakedness. Their faces were turned the other way so that they would not see their father's nakedness (Gen. 9:23).

Shem and Japheth were no doubt disappointed and disgusted with their father. But the respect they showed went beyond the personal. As God covered Adam and Eve's nakedness after the fall, so these boys covered their father's nakedness after his. It was a respect for their father's standing. He had let himself go but he was still their father and the office of father is, by itself, worthy of respect. They literally covered up their father's unfortunate lapse of good taste and decency. And they were commended for it.

Our parents' lack of manners or charm does not relieve us of our responsibility towards them. It becomes us not only to overlook and forgive but even to cover for them in a way that protects their dignity. Our parents are our business.

B. Honour minus zero: no upper age limit

Some things, like dummies or Teletubbies, are just for the kids. We hope our children will outgrow them. Other things, while suitable for children, have a 'U' certificate: Wallace and Grommit, for example, have universal appeal.

When God gave his summary of the very best way to live, ten rules for a just and happy society, he included this one:

> Honour your father and mother, so that you may live long in the land your God is giving you (Exod. 20:12).

So, the menu has something for the kids: adultery and idolatry might be hard to explain, but this one is right where they are. Is that the way we are to read this commandment?

It is certainly correct to make that application. The apostle Paul directly addresses children in his letter to the Ephesians:

> Children, obey your parents in the Lord, for this is right. 'Honour your father and mother' – which is the first commandment with a promise – 'that it may go well with you and that you may enjoy long life on the earth' (Eph. 6:1-3).

Every sensible parent will nod vehemently in agreement and put policies in place which will ensure this happens. And so should every thinking citizen. Isn't it in the interests of all of us that children are taught to respect authority and do as they are told? We can already see the evidence and the consequences of the neglect of this wise command if we are brave enough to walk about our town and city centres on a Friday or Saturday night.

But is that the only application of the fourth command-ment? Is it just in there for the kids or is it 'U' certificate – one for all of us. There is nothing in the Exodus list to suggest that this is the kiddies' corner. It comes between the command about the Lord's day and the one about murder. These are for all of us. As long as we have parents, our behaviour and attitude towards them is to be characterised by honour. The verb 'to honour' is defined as 'to hold in esteem', 'to respect'.

Just as all of us of would, by choice, prefer to live in a community where children know how to behave around adults, surely we would also want to live in a community where we do not hear of elderly people neglected or abandoned whether in geriatric wards, in their own homes or on the hard shoulder of a motorway. But it happens in our world now. And we are rightly appalled.

How wise are God's commands. He has put a system in place to take care of elderly people in the community and that system is the family. Where that fails or disappears, of course there should be a safety net, but the first and best plan is the family.

In a moving essay on this subject, the American writer Walter Wangerin writes:

> The commandments have not expired. Nor have the holy promises that attend them been abolished.
> When, therefore, I am asked regarding the future of some human community, some family, some nation, – or the church, the visible church itself! – straightway I look for obedience to the commands of God. Particularly I wonder regarding the one which urges honor for the parents: I look to see whether someone is singing songs to his aged mother – and if I can find him, I say, 'The signs are good.'

This is no joke. The best prognostication for the life of any community – whether it shall be long or short – is not financial, political, demographic, or even theological. It is moral. Ask not, 'How strong is this nation?' nor 'How many are they? How well organized? With what armies and resources?' Ask rather, 'How does this people behave?'…..

Do we as a people honor our mothers and our fathers? Do we honor the generation that raised us – especially when it sinks down into an old and seemingly dishonorable age? When our parents twist and bow and begin to stink, what then? When they harden in crankiness, what then? Do we by esteeming them make them sweet and lovely again? The question is not irrelevant to our future, whether we shall have one or not. That it may be well with you and you may live long on the earth.

Extract from *This Earthly Pilgrimage* by Walter Wangerin

If to honour our parents when we are children means to obey them, what does it mean when we are past middle age and have raised children of our own?

Matthew Henry, writing in the early eighteenth century, suggested in his comments on Exodus 20:12 that it means:

'Endeavouring in everything to be the comfort of their old age and to make their old age easy to them.'

C. Pops and robbers

The book of Proverbs has a way of graphically depicting in just a sentence or two how living God's way, or not, looks in real life.

On the subject of attitude to parents, these are typical of its warnings:

He who robs his father and drives out his mother is a son who brings shame and disgrace (Prov. 19:26).

There are those who curse their fathers and do not bless their mothers; those who are pure in their own eyes and yet are not cleansed of their filth; those whose eyes are ever so haughty, whose glances are so disdainful; those whose teeth are swords and whose jaws are set with knives to devour the poor from the earth, the needy from among mankind…..

The eye that mocks a father, that scorns obedience to a mother, will be pecked out by the ravens of the valley, will be eaten by the vultures (Prov. 30:11-14, 17).

There are more ways of cursing a parent than by using profanities; there are more ways of robbing a parent than by donning a balaclava and emptying the sideboard of priceless antiques.

A polite way of doing it is beautifully described by Jane Austen:

'It was my father's last request to me,' replied her husband, 'that I should assist his widow and daughters … A hundred a year would make them all perfectly comfortable.'

His wife hesitated a little, however, in giving her consent to this plan.

'To be sure,' said she, it is better than parting with fifteen hundred pounds at once. But then if Mrs Dashwood should live fifteen years we shall be completely taken in.'

'Fifteen years! My dear Fanny; her life cannot be worth half that purchase.'

'Certainly not; but if you observe, people always live for ever when there is an annuity to be paid to them … I have known a great deal of trouble of annuities; for my mother was clogged with the payment of three to old superannuated servants by my father's will, and it is amazing how disagreeable she found it…'

'It certainly is an unpleasant thing,' replied Mr Dashwood, 'to have those kind of yearly drains on one's income ... I believe you are right, my love; it will be better that there should be no annuity in the case; whatever I may give them occasionally will be of far greater assistance than a yearly allowance, because they would only enlarge their style of living if they felt sure of a larger income, and would not be sixpence the richer for it at the end of the year. It will certainly be much the best way. A present of fifty pounds now and then will prevent their ever being distressed for money, and will, I think, be amply discharging my promise to my father.'

'To be sure it will. Indeed, to say the truth, I am convinced within myself that your father had no idea of your giving them any money at all…'

Extract from *Sense and Sensibility* by Jane Austen

How easily we can persuade ourselves of the reasonableness of reducing our liabilities and responsibilities to our ageing and inconvenient parents! It is an expertise we gather during our lives, this passing off neglect of duty until it becomes practically a virtue. – 'Pure in our own eyes' just as the book of Proverbs says in our extract. As for feeling ashamed of ourselves, even the phrase sounds outmoded in these days when self-worth is apparently the '*sine qua non*' of everyday life. Just as the hopeful amateurs on TV singing or dancing contests are cheered and applauded by the audience when they answer back the experts who dare to make a criticism, so when a little voice in our heads asks, 'Is that right? Is that worthy of you?' there are other voices shouting, 'Stand up for yourself. Don't be put upon!'

How telling that one of the most popular catchphrases of this first decade of the twenty-first century 'Am I bovvered? Does this face look bovvered?'

In contrast to such ugly self-assertion and foolish resistance to correction, the book of Proverbs shows us a more excellent way, the way of sustained joy and understanding between the generations. How wonderful and fitting that the baby over whom the besotted parents gasped in wonder at his round cheeks and tiny fingers and toes, should grow to be the mature adult of whom those same parents in their old age can be justly proud.

> Listen to your father who gave you life, and do not despise your mother when she is old. Buy the truth and do not sell it; get wisdom, discipline and understanding. The father of a righteous man has great joy; he who has a wise son delights in him. May your father and mother be glad; may she who gave you birth rejoice! (Prov. 23:22-25).

It may take a deal of wisdom, discipline and understanding, (What is there in this life worth having which doesn't?) but which of these two scenarios is the more attractive: the hunched nodding old man with his chin on his chest forgotten by his family, laughed at by the world, or the same man tenderly smiled upon and treated with dignity even in his pathetic frailty? Which of those two scenes is more fitting for a civilised society?

D. The famous last words
Only John, out of the four gospel writers, records these particular words, probably because they were particularly addressed to him. It has been told that many young soldiers who die on the field of battle cry for their mothers; even condemned prisoners en route to their place of execution sometimes have done the same. In both cases the dying remember with tenderness the comfort that their mothers gave. But when the Son of God

died in excruciating pain greater than this world has ever witnessed, He called to his mother not for his comfort but for hers. At this extreme moment, amongst all the other things he said which were of enormous profundity and theological significance, he made arrangements for the future care of his mother:

> When Jesus saw his mother there, and the disciple whom he loved standing near by, he said to his mother, 'Dear woman, here is your son,' and to the disciple, 'Here is your mother.' From that time on, this disciple took her into his home (John 19:26, 27).

Surely this is a rebuke to all who are so taken up with absorbing occupations, that they have no time to pay attention to their aged parents. The care of his mother, even at this point in his life, was Jesus' concern. If ever a man had the excuse of urgent business, Jesus had it then. But yet the Son of God indicates where our duty and priority lies. How dare we come with our paltry excuses for our neglect of our parents.

The occasion of these words underlines that caring for elderly parents must be deemed a very high priority indeed.

E. Practical Religion

There are those old people whose children predecease them; there are those who have no children. Throughout the Bible the needs of such are presented as close to God's heart; he is the defender of the defenceless and he expects the people who bear his name to be similarly concerned.

> He defends the cause of the fatherless and the widow, and loves the alien, giving him food and clothing (Deut. 10:18).

The New Testament church, full of the Holy Spirit, active in evangelism, was from its earliest days also committed to caring for the needy. There was a daily distribution of food by the church to widows, who would have been without any other means of support. (Acts 6:1).

But in case there were any slacker offspring who thought that it was the business of the church and not them to sort out poor old Mum, the apostle Paul clarified responsibilities.

> Give proper recognition to those widows who are really in need. But if a widow has children or grandchildren, these should learn first of all to put their religion into practice by caring for their own family and so repaying their parents and grandparents, for this is pleasing to God…
>
> If anyone does not provide for his relatives, and especially for his immediate family, he has denied the faith and is worse than an unbeliever (1 Tim. 5:3-4, 8).

From this pithy instruction we deduce (if we haven't already got the message from the rest of this chapter):

- That it really is our business before it is anyone else's, to make sure that the needs of our aged parents are met.
- That we should not shirk the duty of meeting those needs ourselves out of our own funds of money, time and energy.
- That this is as much an expression of trust in Christ as church on Sunday and prayer meeting on Thursday.
- Perhaps even more so, because it is costly and shows we take God's word and ways seriously.
- We owe this to our parents.

- This repayment is therefore required more seriously than that of any student loan.
- When we attempt to do this we please God, who is very interested in the way we treat our parents.
- To refuse to even attempt to pay this debt is tantamount to saying 'I don't believe in Jesus'.
- If even some unbelievers, by common grace, recognise their duty to their parents, believers who have received such special and wonderful grace from God should not be seen to be slacking in this regard.

2

JUST THE JOB

In which I explain why Christians should be better at caring for the elderly than anyone else.

Some jobs are just not made for Christians. For obvious reasons burglary is an occupation totally unsuitable; pole-dancing would be equally so. On the other hand most legal and decent jobs present opportunities along the way to demonstrate Christian virtues like honesty, industry, reliability or compassion.

But caring for an elderly relative or neighbour is as fitting for the Christian as the glass slipper for Cinderella. When Prince Charming comes along with the slipper on its velvet cushion, it is soon apparent that those ugly crones of sisters are not going to be able to wedge their great feet in. But the glass slipper goes on Cinderella's foot as if it were made for her, which of course it was.

This chapter aims to show that caring for an elderly parent is not only right, it is eminently suitable work for someone who claims to be a follower of Jesus Christ. The job profile matches perfectly.

Furthermore, just as the fitting of the glass slipper identified Cinderella as the prince's bride (cue: wedding bells) so this particular kind of work of service identifies those who are rightly called the bride of Christ, those who are being made ready for the great wedding supper as described in Revelation 19:6-8.

This kind of work is a perfect showcase for what God is about and what his people therefore should be about. Here are six reasons why Christians ought to be better at doing this than anyone else.

A. Money cannot buy it

I know I have touched on this before, but in these days when blatant self-interest is expected without apology or embarrassment, doing something 'for love', as my mother used to say, makes an impact. To borrow from Shakespeare, it is the good deed which shines in a naughty world. Those who of their own free will sneak out with the Ajax and a scrubbing brush to clean obscene graffiti off the subway walls might be thought seriously weird by those who hurry by to catch a train, but they make our communities a better place to be and most people are grudgingly grateful to them. Similarly, those who give of their time to hold an old lady's hand and listen to her stories, or who push an old man out in his wheelchair to the park so that he can watch the cricket, enhance the society in which we live. They do us all a service by making our towns and cities more humane.

There is, for those who spend more than thirty-five hours a week caring for an elderly person, a state benefit, but don't get excited: this is a token recognition. Giving up paid employment to care for your mother will never be a great career move. In 2006 this 'Carer's Allowance' amounted to approximately £45 a week. I believe that is what union leaders in the good old nineteen-seventies would have called a derisory offer. So those who do this could not possibly be doing it for the money.

But, aside from the question of whether the state should come down more handsomely in recognition of those who sacrificially contribute to the welfare of old people, we find in this the rather heartening thought that the principle of self-interest does not have to rule our lives and that the lives of all of us are enriched by something which will not appear on any bank statement.

This is the image of God who invites the spiritually and morally destitute to eat and drink at his restaurant at his expense:

> Come, all you who are thirsty, come to the waters; and you who have no money, come, buy and eat! Come, buy wine and milk without money and without cost. Why spend money on what is not bread, and your labour on what does not satisfy? Listen, listen to me and eat what is good, and your soul will delight in the richest of fare. Give ear and come to me; hear me, that your soul may live. I will make an everlasting covenant with you, my faithful love promised to David (Isa. 55:1-3).

Money cannot buy peace with God, forgiveness of sins, entry to heaven or everlasting life but God freely offers these things. He so loved the world.

When we attempt to clear up the mess others have made, or when we love the unlovely, we demonstrate the kind of weirdness God likes. We give the lie to the evolutionary survival of the fittest maxim; we demonstrate that humankind is in a class of its own, a little lower than the angels, a feeble but still real reflection of the God who made us.

B. It cannot be reciprocated

Much of life operates on a quid pro quo arrangement. I babysit your kids, you babysit mine. We exchange Christmas cards and invitations to dinner.

But if you visit an old lady or scrub her step or fetch her shopping, it is not part of the deal that she will do these things for you. As a matter of fact that sometimes presents a problem to the recipient of the good deed. The old lady fumbles with her purse and tries to press a crumpled £5 note in your hand. You leave it on the coffee table. It is humbling to be unable to reciprocate. It doesn't do anything for one's pride. Perhaps that is the point of old age: to underline the fact that despite all that we may achieve when we are in our prime, at a fundamental level we cannot manage on our own. The fall has crippled us all incurably and we need more than a Zimmer frame to lean on.

The gospel of Jesus Christ is a non-reciprocal arrangement. We do nothing, Jesus has done everything; he gives, we receive.

> Nothing in my hand I bring,
> Simply to thy cross I cling;
> Naked, come to thee for dress,
> Helpless, look to thee for grace.
> Foul I to the fountain fly:
> Wash me, Saviour, or I die
>> Extract from *Rock of Ages* by Augustus Toplady

So, again caring for the elderly is God's kind of work precisely because they cannot reciprocate.

Jesus once made the point at a dinner party.

Then Jesus said to his host, 'When you give a luncheon or dinner, do not invite your friends, your brothers or relatives, or your rich neighbours; if you do, they may invite you back and so you will be repaid. But when you give a banquet, invite the poor, the crippled, the lame, the blind, and you will be blessed. Although they cannot repay you, you will be repaid at the resurrection of the righteous' (Luke 14:12 14).

C. It is lowly work
When I commenced caring for my father-in-law, I was introduced to the brave new world of catheters and dentures; but as a shock to my sensitive soul and sheltered existence, that was nothing compared to the frequent experience of clearing up excrement. Life at its extreme end is reduced to very basic things. I never thought that a person's bowels could feature so large in my life.

People told me that I was very noble in caring for my father-in-law. But it did not feel noble; it felt demeaning. Although it is wonderful to be able to make an old man clean, fragrant and comfortable, only someone with no sense of smell could call the job pleasant. And of course it was only a matter of time before the whole process would have to be repeated.

It is lowly work to clean and replace dentures, wipe a dribble from a chin, scrub at a stain on the carpet. Especially to those whose hands are more accustomed to tapping at a computer or turning the pages of a book. Certainly there is no component of caring for an elderly person which would enhance a CV.

This is where an action of Jesus comes strikingly to mind.

It was just before the Passover Feast. Jesus knew that the time had come for him to leave this world and go to the

Father. Having loved his own who were in the world, he now showed them the full extent of his love.

The evening meal was being served, and the devil had already prompted Judas Iscariot, son of Simon, to betray Jesus. Jesus knew that the Father had put all things under his power, and that he had come from God and was returning to God; so he got up from the meal, took off his outer clothing, and wrapped a towel round his waist. After that, he poured water into a basin and began to wash his disciples' feet, drying them with the towel that was wrapped round him (John 13:1-5).

What a strange juxtaposition is this, that at a point when Jesus was as sure as he had ever been of who he was and where he was heading, he stripped off and did the work of a slave. The King of Kings was not demeaned by service of the lowliest kind. It is precisely what he was about. His very coming to the world was an immeasurable step down. His hands regularly touched the unclean; he mixed with people from the bad side of town by choice; and when the foot-washing occurred he was only hours away from an ignominious death. Learn and imitate, says the apostle Paul:

Your attitude should be the same as that of Christ Jesus:

Who, being in very nature God,
    did not consider equality with God something to be
        grasped,
but made himself nothing,
    taking the very nature of a servant,
    being made in human likeness.
And being found in appearance as a man,
    He humbled himself
    and became obedient to death – even death on
        a cross! (Phil. 2:6-8).

Practical, basic care is as truly Christian work as teaching Sunday school or preaching a sermon. Some would argue that the lowlier the deed of service, the more likeness to the Master.

D. It is hidden work
The man who stands up and preaches the gospel is visible to all; even the one who serves the tea will be seen.

Deeds of kindness can be public: charity concerts and auctions can make generosity a publicity stunt. Pink Floyd did themselves no harm by performing at Live8 for free.

But looking after old people is hidden work: only they know and they may well forget:

'I haven't seen a soul all day.'
'But didn't I just see the district nurse drive away?'

But these are the kind of secrets God likes. Visiting an old person is a kind of giving and Jesus' take on giving was that it worked best as a clandestine activity:

'Be careful not to do your "acts of righteousness" before men, to be seen by them. If you do, you will have no reward from your father in heaven. So when you give to the needy, do not announce it with trumpets, as the hypocrites do in the synagogues and on the streets, to be honoured by men. I tell you the truth, they have received their reward in full. But when you give to the needy, do not let your left hand know what your right hand is doing, so that your giving may be in secret. Then your father, who sees what is done in secret, will reward you' (Matt. 6:1-4).

Most of us will not make a name for ourselves; we will not be remembered on earth one generation on. But our secret deeds will have made a difference and our Father will have seen them and smiled.

The last sentence of George Eliot's novel *Middlemarch* pays tribute to those whose goodness is expressed behind closed doors:

> '... the growing good of the world is partly dependent on unhistoric acts; and that things are not so ill with you and me as they might have been, is half owing to the number who lived faithfully a hidden life, and rest in unvisited tombs.'

> Extract from *Middlemarch* by George Eliot.

When the untold story of the universe is revealed, and God's faithful collect their crowns in glory, those with the most amazing crowns will not be the ones who had most votes from the viewers. They are likely to be ones we never even noticed, who faithfully showed their love for Christ in lowly works of service, and not a soul knew about it.

They follow the pattern of the unseen God, whose power and love keeps the world turning and yet whose gracious provision is unacknowledged by the majority of the world's inhabitants.

E. It uses our gifts

I do not mean by this that in caring for old Dad anyone will find an outlet for the gift of playing the saxophone or in preaching. On the contrary, I was frequently all too well aware that I was being asked to do things which were way outside of my gifting, training or experience.

'I'm a teacher, not a nurse,' I sometimes muttered to myself as I emptied urine out of a catheter bag.

But there is a much more significant gift which all Christians have received. That gift is the love of God the

Father lavished on us through our Lord Jesus Christ. We have received the comfort of the gospel, whereby we who were God's enemies are adopted into his family. Not only so, in the troubles which face us in this life, God helps and comforts his people. Now when God gives those gifts they have not reached their terminus. The living water is to flow out in a gushing stream not be dammed up. Paul writes to the Corinthians:

> Praise be to the God and Father of our Lord Jesus Christ, the Father of compassion and the God of all comfort, who comforts us in all our troubles, so that we can comfort those in any trouble with the comfort we ourselves have received from God (2 Cor. 1:3-4).

The point is that we are supposed to pass these things on. The cupboard is full with all that we have received: the deep love of Jesus, comfort in our troubles. So, we of all people are wonderfully resourced to give comfort to our parents in their declining years.

F. It respects the image of God
The ghastliest aspect of old age is the loss of dignity. It is what we all fear. Yet again it points to the fact that we are quite distinct from the animal kingdom. We know that despite the decrepitude and incapacities of our bodies we have significance. There is something of us which stands apart from our sagging frames and says 'but that is not me'.

Each one of us is made in God's image; each one is a living soul. To treat with tenderness and respect the ageing body of an elderly neighbour or relative is fitting because of what that body houses. Such a treatment is not born of sentimentality, because the person concerned is 'a dear', although that may be the case. The motive for care and concern for elderly people is that each one is made in the image of God. And though time and wear and tear has made some of these folks unattractive or cantankerous, they still are worthy of respect because they remain God's creation and bear his image.

It was this thought, drawn wholly from the pages of the Bible, that drove Lord Shaftesbury to work tirelessly for the poor during the nineteenth century. He did not put an end to the practice of sending small boys and girls up chimneys because he loved children and thought they were cute. He did it because he understood how precious each one was as a bearer of God's image

To give time and effort and money to enhance the comfort and well-being of the elderly dignifies them. Evolutionary thought would consign old people to the scrap heap of humanity. They have, according to that worldview, fulfilled their only useful purpose on this earth by reproducing themselves. So they can be left to rot, literally or metaphorically. But the worldview which acknowledges a Creator God is appalled by such an attitude. Old people, all people, are worthy of respect because they are immortal souls, made by God for his glory.

These high-sounding ideals actually work their way out in little things. In her diatribe against the rudeness of everyday life, Lynne Truss cites this instance:

> People who have spent their whole lives as 'Mr Webster' or 'Mrs Owen' do not want to find at the ends of their lives, that younger people who don't know them are calling them 'Alf' and 'Joyce'. To them it is sheer impertinence (and usually takes place when they are in a weakened state, which makes it all the more insensitive).
>
> Extract from *Talk to the Hand* by Lynne Truss

So those who understand that we are in God's image are best placed to do all in their power to respect and restore dignity by loving and sensitive care of their aged parents or friends.

Unbelievers are often to be found engaged in sacrificial care of the type I have been describing. That should not surprise us, for that too is the image of God. Their admirable behaviour is quite irrational and inexplicable from within an atheistic evolutionary framework.

But the Christian has all the more reason and motive to serve in this way. It is almost an enactment of the gospel itself, it is grace: to love and serve those who cannot return the favour, to volunteer for unpleasant tasks for the sake of their welfare. What more fitting work for those who have themselves been the undeserving recipients of such love and grace? What job is more suitable to those who follow the one who died for them?

3

WHAT'S IN IT FOR ME?

*In which I outline the benefits of caring for
an aged parent.*

Aha! The principle of self-interest rears its ugly head after all. But read on. There are certainly gains to be had in caring for an elderly friend or relative, but these are by no means an automatic pay-off. For, the first thing to note about sustained care of this kind is that it is rarely something that any of us would rush towards wholeheartedly as the thing we most wanted to do at this time in our lives. It would not appear in any list of 'twenty things to have done before you're sixty':

16. Climb Kilimanjaro
17. Help Dad get washed and dressed
18. Swim with dolphins

In middle age, many of us are up to our chins in being parents: we might still be supporting our children financially and emotionally. We are also just beginning to enjoy relating to them as adults. Perhaps we are on the threshold of grandparenthood. Demands for an increase in input from us from the other direction, i.e. from our own parents, much as we love them, are as welcome as an income tax self-assessment form. We would always prefer to postpone involvement in favour of more congenial activities.

I think it is best to be honest about this. Perhaps it is because I did 'King Lear' for 'A' level that I have always been deeply suspicious of people who gush about the joy and sense of privilege. The plot of King Lear hangs on the foolish whim of Lear, already an old man at the start of the play, to know which of his three daughters love him best. He plans to share out his kingdom and effects according to how much he likes the answer in each case. Mawkish sentimentality regarding an aged parent puts me in mind of ghastly Goneril, who publicly declares that her selfish and imperious old father is 'dearer than eyesight, space or liberty.' But a few scenes later when both her space and her liberty have been invaded by her father and her eyes have had their fill of his ways, she calls him 'an idle old man' and wants rid of him:

> By day and night he wrongs me: every hour
> He flashes into one gross crime or other,
> That sets us all at odds: I'll not endure it;
> > Extract from *King Lear* by William Shakespeare

No, I'm with Cordelia, the youngest sister, on this one. When her father invites his daughters to engage in this silly but serious competition to 'prove' who loves him most, Cordelia refuses to play:

Good my lord,
You have begot me, bred me, loved me: I
Return those duties back as are right fit,
Obey you, love you and most honour you.

I love your majesty
According to my bond; nor more, nor less.

Extract from *King Lear* by William Shakespeare

According to my bond is exactly it. The basis of our care is that it is right and fitting behaviour by a son or daughter towards a parent. Of course there is room for tenderness, but knowing that you do this because it is right is what will get you through the days when the needle on the tenderness gauge is waggling dangerously near zero. There is great tenderness in Cordelia's parting words to her sisters when they cart off in triumph the aged parent and his money: 'Use well our father,' she says. But we all know that is as likely as Accrington Stanley winning the FA cup.

Part of your story

It rather depends on how you view your life. If you see it in terms of an agenda set by you to experience and achieve things which will always enhance your comfort and happiness, then extra unlooked-for duties at a busy time, can only be seen as an impediment to that agenda.

But what if someone else is setting the agenda and that someone else has something other than your immediate comfort and happiness in view? Our perspective on life is often tragically godless: we automatically put ourselves at the centre. But from start to finish, this is God's universe and his great plan in the universe is to mend what was broken. His redemptive work in sending his Son is the centre of that plan.

At one time we too were foolish, disobedient, deceived and enslaved by all kinds of passions and pleasures. We lived in malice and envy, being hated and hating one another. But when the kindness and love of God our Saviour appeared, he saved us, not because of righteous things we had done, but because of his mercy. He saved us through the washing of rebirth and renewal by the Holy Spirit, whom he poured out on us generously through Jesus Christ our Saviour, so that, having been justified by his grace, we might become heirs having the hope of eternal life (Titus 3:3-7).

So now God is preparing his redeemed people for his kingdom. His agenda for each one of those who have trusted Christ is that we should be repaired. Coming to Christ starts with repentance and this denotes a change of direction in life. But the change is continuous. God changes circumstances in our lives all the time; but he also intends that we should use those circumstances as instruments of change in us, change for the better, change for the holier.

Viewed this way, husbands, wives, children, parents, friends, enemies, neighbours, colleagues, employers and employees, as their paths cross ours, all present us with a challenge. How will we respond to them? Will the relationship make us better people?

God, who oversees the finest details of our lives, has brought the whole cast of thousands, with whom we strut about on life's stage, for a purpose. Where will the interaction lead? Will the curtain come down on a tragedy, with the stage littered with corpses because the hero refuses to learn from life's mistakes and misfortunes?

That is the way of the fool as portrayed in the book of Proverbs.

The way of a fool seems right to him, but a wise man listens to advice (Prov. 12:15).

Though you grind a fool in a mortar, grinding him like grain with a pestle, you will not remove his folly from him (Prov. 27:22).

But God's purpose for his people, for whom Jesus Christ died, is that by allowing the other players to shape their thinking and their behaviour they emerge at the end triumphant. Every believer's life is a redemption story: it comes precariously close to disaster but there is a turn in the road, a distance is travelled, lessons are learnt, the rescue is complete. For believers, God writes comedies (in the classical sense) not tragedies, and every character he writes into the plot has a significant part to play towards that final happy ending, which is likeness to Christ.

And we know that in all things God works for the good of those who love him, who have been called according to his purpose. For those God foreknew he also predestined to be conformed to the likeness of his Son, that he might be the firstborn among many brothers. And those he predestined, he also called; those he called, he also justified; those he justified, he also glorified (Rom. 8:28-30).

A place to grow

So if God was writing a list of twenty experiences for you to face before you are sixty, he might include many delightful events like births and marriages, but, given his overall purpose to make you like Jesus, he is likely to also slip into the plot things like:

16. Teenage daughter comes home tattooed.
17. Mum has a stroke and needs more help and attention.
18. Boss says, 'Clear your desk and leave today.'

Consider it pure joy. It is hard to say that sentence without at least a trace of sarcasm in the voice. But James is not being sarcastic.

> Consider it pure joy, my brothers, whenever you face trials of many kinds, because you know that the testing of your faith develops perseverance. Perseverance must finish its work so that you may be mature and complete, not lacking anything (James 1:2-4).

We throw up our hands and say, 'I could have done without this.' But God has decided precisely the opposite. He has decided that this trial from which we shrink is just what we need. It is a necessary condition for our growth to maturity.

This will not happen automatically, however. Suffering does not ennoble by itself. You may have noticed that suffering frequently embitters people.

This is how trials (otherwise known as suffering, difficulty or trouble) work.

1. Trials present us with a mirror

Take kindness, for example. That is a fruit that the Holy Spirit wants to grow in the life of every believer.

I used to think I was a kind person until I was faced with a person whose demands on me were inconvenient. It is easy to be kind at your own convenience. Here is a blind person who needs help to cross the road. I am walking by and it is really no trouble at all to stop and see her safely across. She says, 'Thank you so much.' I say, 'You're welcome.' We both go on our way rejoicing, especially me because I have just enhanced my self-image by doing this little good deed. I am so thrilled there are tears in my eyes at my own beautiful gesture.

But here is a blind person whom I get to know a little better. Her needs are immense, not just for practical help but for emotional support. And she needs it regularly. And I find I am less thrilled because there are a hundred more interesting things, even important things, than picking up the stitches she has dropped in the dishcloth she is knitting while listening to her piteous tale of familiar neglect. I find, in short that I am not as kind as I liked to believe myself. Although I might do these things and do them regularly I am doing them in a kind of fury. I know that I am being sucked in and I fear being swallowed up. And even while I might be inwardly sighing or muttering under my breath, the Holy Spirit is saying to me, 'Look at yourself; listen to yourself. It's not pretty.' And I have to face the fact that one thing I am not, is kind.

Now this whole situation is a learning opportunity. But it starts with the exposure of my true self, or at least, as much of it as I can stand at any one time. Relationships and circumstances reveal our hearts especially when those relationships and circumstances are not to our liking.

2. Trials present us with a choice

To decide to get actively or more intimately involved with the care of an aged parent presents us with the opportunity to enrol in the school of kindness, or patience, or meekness, or compassion. Will we see it that way? Or will we choose instead self-pity? If we take the self-pity option, even though we may do the necessary for our parents, we will reap no growth for ourselves. We will not graduate with anything but an embittered or martyr spirit.

All of life's situations have at least two handles. And we have to take care to choose the right one. In his letter, James continues on the theme of trials in the Christian life by looking at the example of poverty and riches.

The brother in humble circumstances ought to take pride in his high position. But the one who is rich should take pride in his low position, because he will pass away like a wild flower (James 1:9-10).

A poor person has a choice between envy and thankfulness, between a carnal attitude which sets huge store on the riches you can see, and a spiritual attitude which knows that the important things are the unseen ones. A rich person has a choice between thinking that he is better than other people, or realising that the truth is that his riches do not gain him any standing with God and that his need for salvation is as great as any man's alive. It is not the riches or the poverty that make people better people it is the response they choose to make to the riches or the poverty which is crucial.

Someone who in late middle age faces the burden of care for a frail parent has a choice between resentment at feeling lumbered and compassion for one who is so unwillingly dependent.

Every 'yes' to compassion and 'no' to self-pity, even where there is a struggle (and there will be if the situation continues), is a learning of a lesson in the school of kindness. It is a keeping in step with the Spirit. It is a step on the road not to encumbrance but to liberty. It is another nail in the coffin of the sinful nature.

You, my brothers, were called to be free. But do not use your freedom to indulge the sinful nature; rather serve one another in love.

But the fruit of the Spirit is love, joy peace, patience, kindness, goodness, faithfulness, gentleness and self-control. Against such things there is no law. Those who belong to Christ Jesus have crucified the sinful nature with its passions and desires. Since we live by the Spirit, let us keep in step with the Spirit (Gal. 5:13, 22-25).

3. Trials present us with a need
James predicts this because he follows up his command to look on trials positively with these words:

> If any of you lacks wisdom, he should ask God, who gives generously to all without finding fault, and it will be given to him (James 1:5).

We need wisdom because otherwise we will not use our sorrows well. We need help to face up to ourselves, we need help to make the right choice. But help is there.

Did you ever, as a child at school, approach the teacher's desk with a muddle of arithmetic and ask for help. Sometimes the first thing you got was a telling off for not paying proper attention and making such elementary mistakes. Added to which you had omitted to write the date and draw a margin.

God is not like that kind of teacher. He does not turn away requests for help nor give it grudgingly or with a telling off for being so puny. When our troubles drive us to God, they do us a big, big favour. They send us to someone who is glad to help.

Practice makes not quite perfect
One of our boys wanted to learn the trombone. Now the trombone is a beautiful piece of work, very shiny and shapely. And what greater fun can be imagined than manoeuvring with precision that slide and making that oom-pah-pah sound. But if you have ever tried even to get a sound out of a trombone you will know that this is not

going to be a short-term project. For weeks the only sound to be heard during trombone practice in our house was a concerto which our daughter named 'Man on a toilet'. This is a painful stage in trombone playing which cannot be avoided in the early days. There is no shirking it. You only get to play a trombone well via playing it badly. You do not get anywhere by merely admiring the instrument nestling cosily in its case.

Now learning patience or kindness is like that. You don't learn to be kind by thinking or reading about it. You have to practise. And if you have ever prayed asking God to help you to be kind, or to make you kinder, do not be surprised if pretty soon across your path falls the shadow of one of the least deserving and most demanding of the human species, on whom you can practise. And you will make a mess of it plenty of times. But if you will persevere there will be progress.

Similarly with patience. In God's school of patience there are very few dear sweet biddable people to handle. You wouldn't learn much patience around those. Instead there are cantankerous and grumpy ones, who drive you nuts. But keep practising. Listen to yourself, look at yourself, make the right choice of response, ask for help continually. You won't ever reach perfection, but you are getting there.

One of my favourite of Charles Dickens' characters comes from the novel *Martin Chuzzlewit*. His name is Mark Tapley and he is a work of fiction. But he is an inspiring one.

Mark Tapley makes it his aim to be jolly. His view is that when he is around pleasant people there is no credit in being jolly: that is far too easy. No. Mark sets himself the challenge of being jolly around objectionable people. He leaves his happy situation at 'The Dragon' where he is much liked by the patrons and by the charming landlady Mrs Lupin, because, as he puts it:

I'm always a-thinking that with my good health and spirits it would be more creditable in me to be jolly when there's things a-going on to make one dismal.

Extract from *Martin Chuzzlewit* by Charles Dickens

When Martin Chuzzlewit, a selfish young puppy, decides to go to America to try and make his fortune, although he is spectacularly naïve and ill-equipped to do so, Mark Tapley insists on going with him as his (unpaid) manservant.

Here I am with a liking for what's wentersome, and a liking for you, and a wish to come out strong under circumstances as would keep other men down: will you take me..?

Now that you've said America, I see clear at once, that that's the place for me to be jolly in.

Extract from *Martin Chuzzlewit* by Charles Dickens

So better than climbing Kilimanjaro is the adventure of learning to be kind, or patient, or gentle or self-controlled in circumstances that would drive other men and women over the edge. Not because you are better than others or naturally kinder or more patient etc., but because you have a great coach in God the Holy Spirit. And the credit, where there is credit, goes to him not to you. Which gives you even more reason to be jolly.

So to sum up, the best response to trials is to embrace them. And if that trial comes in the form of an aged parent, brace yourself for some training in kindness, patience, meekness, gentleness and self-control and thank God for the opportunity to enrol in his school with the best of all trainers at your side.

4

WHAT IS IT LIKE TO BE OLD?

In which I attempt to explore the ageing experience from the inside.

'Don't get old,' my father-in-law remarked on frequent occasions as we supported his tottering steps or placed his tablets into his quivering hand.

I never quite worked out the correct reply to that instruction:

'Do you mean you want me to die young?'

But I realise now that was merely his way of expressing what a very difficult journey ageing is. In the vernacular, 'you don't want to go there!'

So, in a book about caring for elderly parents, it is important to spend some time considering what it is like for them. What are they experiencing?

There is hardly a truer sentence in the English language than, 'You don't know what I'm going through.' None of us can ever truly know how it feels to stand in someone else's shoes and see with their eyes and feel their pain. We can observe but then appearances can deceive; we can listen but then people are often very limited in their ability to express; so perhaps we need that under-used gift of God: our imagination.

One way in which we can be helped in this work of the imagination is by a survey of literature. A good writer is proficient at expressing how it is for other people. A good writer gets inside people's skins. As a graduate in psychology, I maintain that you can learn more about the way human beings operate from the writings of Shakespeare, Milton, Austen or Dickens than from any psychology textbook.

So this chapter will draw more than ever from works of literature as we take a ride through the ageing experience.

A. The ageing experience

My survey boils it down to four, the four challenges of old age: foolishness, feebleness, frustration and fear.

1. Foolishness

If you have ever tripped up a kerb and fallen onto your hands and knees in the middle of the high street full of shoppers on a Saturday morning, you know about feeling a fool. People are kind and help you up and ask you if you are all right and you say 'yes' because your only thought is to get away from there as fast as possible. Your hand is grazed but your pride is smashed to smithereens. It is extremely embarrassing as a grown-up to look as helpless and vulnerable as a child.

That is how it is all the time for the man who discovers that he has dribbled his drink, for the woman who cannot get up out of her chair – which are both everyday experiences for the elderly. He feels a fool to be unable to change a lightbulb; she feels a ninny to be unable to put her own tights on. But there is nowhere to run to, no place to hide. The continual awareness of your own ineptitude is something you have to live with.

The humiliation can begin in middle age with the 'can't find my glasses' conundrum:

> You spend your time taking off your seeing glasses to put on your reading glasses, and then remembering that your reading glasses are upstairs or in the car,
>   And then you can't find your seeing glasses again because without them you can't see where they are.
>   Extract from *Peekaboo, I almost see you* by Ogden Nash

But losing or rather misplacing things is a regular event in old age. So is the forgetting what has happened in the recent past. Sometimes a person may be blissfully unaware that she has asked the same question of the same person several times in the last quarter of an hour. (It is a kindness to preserve their ignorance on this point and I have found the tedium can be abated by giving a different answer each time.) But often the foolishness is all too disconcertingly evident to everyone and coming to terms with it is a long hard struggle.

At the height of his humiliation King Lear makes this poignant admission:

> Pray do not mock me:
> I am a very foolish, fond old man,
> Fourscore and upward, not an hour more nor less,
> And, to deal plainly,
> I fear I am not in my perfect mind,
> Methinks I should know you, and know this man;
> Yet I am doubtful: for I am mainly ignorant
> What place this is; and all the skill I have

Remembers not these garments; nor do I know
Where I did lodge last night.
> Extract from *King Lear* by William Shakespeare

2. Feebleness

Alongside the sense of foolishness is the sense of increasing weakness. Actions which were once performed expertly without a thought now cannot be done at all without aid of some kind. Faculties are failing: vision, co-ordination, mobility, hearing. Some manoeuvres are painful and all of them are slower. The Bible includes this graphic and poetic description of the last stage of life:

Remember your Creator in the days of your youth, before the days of trouble come and the years approach when you will say, 'I find no pleasure in them' –

Before the sun and the light and the moon and the stars grow dark, and the clouds return after the rain; when the keepers of the house tremble, and the strong men stoop, when the grinders cease because they are few, and those looking through the windows grow dim; when the doors to the street are closed and the sound of grinding fades; when men rise up at the sound of birds, but all their songs grow faint; when men are afraid of heights and of dangers in the streets; when the almond tree blossoms and the grasshopper drags himself along and desire no longer is stirred.

Then man goes to his eternal home and mourners go about the streets (Eccles. 12:1-5).

In his series of *Talking Heads* monologues, Alan Bennett gave an insight into the thought-lives of a range of people, many of them elderly. Doris, memorably played by Thora Hird, found herself on the floor and unable to get up:

It's such a silly thing to have done. I should never have tried to dust. Zulima says to me every time she comes, 'Doris, do not attempt to dust; the dusting is my department. That's what the council pay me for. You are now a lady of leisure; your dusting days are over.'

Which would be all right provided she did dust, but Zulima doesn't dust. She half-dusts. I know when a place isn't clean. When she's going, she says, 'Doris, I don't want to hear that you've been touching the Ewbank. The Ewbank is out of bounds.'

I say, 'I could just run round with it now and again.'

She says, 'You can't run anywhere…'

Extract from *Talking Heads* by Alan Bennett

Just in case you are not aware how very feeble you are, there are people ready to tell you about it all day long. They mean it kindly with all this talk of taking it easy but the subtext concerning your incapability is dismaying.

3. Frustration

All of us need to feel useful in some way; all of us like to feel included. But what if the feebleness of one's frame or the diminishing of one's faculties prevents one from accessing the full cupboard of life?

The blind old woman sewing alone in her flat drops her needle; she then spends all evening on her hands and knees feeling the carpet.

The old lady sits amongst friends and family at a restaurant looking about her in a bemused fashion. There is a lot of talking and laughter but it is coming from different directions thick and fast and her hearing is not what it was. She cannot follow the conversation; she cannot join in the joke.

The old man gazes out of the window of his flat. It is a beautiful day, but his legs will not carry him more than a few steps, leaning heavily on a frame. And who is there to push his heavy wheelchair?

Each of the above situations contributes to a huge sense of being side-lined, of having no part to play in the world. Arnold Bennett in *The Old Wives' Tale* describes Constance at the end of her days as feeling 'that the tide of life had left her stranded in utter neglect'. She is well cared for and not without means, but in her old age she feels incarcerated. Confined by sciatica to her sofa, her world has shrunk to the size of her parlour. She is now obliged to watch others do things for her less well than she used to do them herself. And she is supposed to be grateful. Like Doris, in Alan Bennett's piece quoted above, she is scathing of contemporary standards but unable to do a thing about it. So, to spare her pain or disgust, and to spare themselves her disapproval, those who surround her keep her in the dark about many things and this serves in turn to further isolate her from the real world. So the spiral of uselessness and frustration grows.

As W. H. Auden put it, 'Who can bear to feel himself forgotten?'

4. Fear

There is the ultimate fear, the fear of death, for despite infirmity and difficulties of every kind, human beings, made for eternity, mostly cling to life, raging against the 'dying of the light'. But as a person gets older, the inevitability of demise is harder to deny:

> Deep in myself I felt a sense of doom
> Fearful of death I trudge towards the tomb
>> Extract from *Chelsea 1977* by John Betjeman

However, it is not just death but life which is scary.

Feebleness and foolishness has robbed the older person of confidence. So there is fear of officials in uniform, fear of young people in hoodies, fear of knocks at the door, fear of uneven pavements, fear of new technology, fear of doctors, fear of constipation, fear of being caught short, fear of foreigners, fear of food poisoning, fear of catching a cold, fear of noises at night, fear of not being ready, fear of offending the neighbours, fear of upsetting the family. The list goes on and on.

This collection of fears, trivial or serious, real or imagined, typically manifests itself in a fussiness over details. Jane Austen's creation, Mr Woodhouse, the elderly father of Emma in the book of that title, is a classic illustration of the nervousness of old age.

> His spirits required support. He was a nervous man, easily depressed; fond of everybody that he was used to, and hating to part with them; hating change of every kind. Matrimony, as the origin of change, was always disagreeable; and he was by no means reconciled to his daughter's marrying ...
>
> Extract from *Emma* by Jane Austen

The focus of his anxiety might be something as innocuous as a portrait in which the subject is dressed in flimsy clothes and might catch a chill, or the circulation of wedding-cake, which he found a source of great distress:

> His own stomach could bear nothing rich, and he could never believe other people to be different from himself. What was unwholesome to him, he regarded as unfit for any body; and he had, therefore, earnestly tried to dissuade them from having any wedding-cake at all, and

when that proved vain, as earnestly tried to prevent any body's eating it. He had been at the pains of consulting Mr Perry, the apothecary, on the subject. Mr Perry was an intelligent, gentleman-like man, whose frequent visits were one of the comforts of Mr Woodhouse's life; and, upon being applied to, he could not but acknowledge, (though it seemed rather against the bias of inclination,) that wedding-cake might certainly disagree with many – perhaps with most people, unless taken moderately. With such an opinion, in confirmation of his own, Mr Woodhouse hoped to influence every visitor of the newly-married pair; but still the cake was eaten; and there was no rest for his benevolent nerves till it was all gone.

Extract from *Emma* by Jane Austen

B. The coping mechanisms

How do we handle our experiences? We choose, unconsciously most of the time, a strategy which enables us to cope. And that is the face we present to the world. So, out of these experiences of foolishness, feebleness, frustration and fear comes an old person's response. This is relevant because this response is what the carer is dealing with and it can sometimes mask the real problem.

It is this response which can strain a relationship. One can sympathise with the foolish, support the feeble, encourage the frustrated and reassure the fearful and do those things with a degree of tenderness, at least on good days.

When those experiences are overlaid with an unattractive, charmless response, like anger or self-pity, then the carer is tested. Our parents are sinners like ourselves; they do not always choose the best handle on a situation. Here are a typical range of coping mechanisms.

1. Fussiness

When, with increasing age, so much is beyond a person's control, elderly people are inclined to greedily obsess over what lies within their dominion. They become incomprehensibly fussy over details. They are ready and sitting in their coats an hour before the taxi is due to arrive. They must get home early in order to put the binbag out. They worry over the irregularity of their bowels.

Margaret Forster has created an accurate portrait of how fear translates itself into fussiness and nervousness in her book, *Mother, can you hear me*. In this extract Angela, in response to her parents' complaint that they never go anywhere, has taken her elderly parents on holiday.

Mother and Father began packing to go home the night before the second-last day.

'Might as well do it now,' Mother said, 'then it's done.'

'No sense hanging about,' Father said, 'start early and we'll have plenty of time to do it. No hurry.'

'The week isn't over yet,' Angela said, exasperated into the reaction he wanted. 'We have two whole days left. Why spoil those two days packing?'

'Doesn't spoil them,' Father said.

'Of course it does – all this thinking ahead instead of enjoying the present.'

'Oh, you have to think ahead,' Father said, 'get things done in time and that. We'd be in a mess otherwise, wouldn't we, Mam?'

'Would we?' Mother said, but she was as bad as he was, always hurrying on to the next thing, constantly clearing quite clear decks.

'That case could be packed in five minutes,' Angela said, 'there just isn't any need to do it now.'

'We aren't clever like you Angela,' Mother said, 'it takes us longer. We're old and slow.'

'Oh don't be so ridiculous,' Angela said angrily, 'it's got nothing to do with being either old or slow. It's an attitude to life.'

Extract from *Mother can you hear me?* by Margaret Forster

2. Self-pity

'Nobody listens. Nobody takes me seriously. Nobody does anything for me. The doctor came, just looked and went away – didn't do a thing.'

'I'm just stuck here in this chair. I never go anywhere. No one's got time for me. They're all rushing about busy with their own things.'

'I've wasted my life.'

Self-pity is a response to a perception of one's own feebleness. It puts out a challenge to the listener to argue the point but it is happy in the confidence that it will not be gainsaid. Because if you, the listener, start off along the 'count-your-blessings' line, you are merely proving the point that you don't listen and you don't know what it's like.

Self-pity embraces victim status like a blanket and is triumphant in its misery.

Like Alice's tears, it can turn into an ocean which all but drowns.

3. Anger
Anger is the classic response to frustration. Throw all the toys out of the cot. Kick the cat. Grumble and rant about everything. Rage is at least an activity in which you can

thoroughly participate in from your armchair. That is why there are so many grumpy old men and grumpy old women. It can be amusing when directed at the vagaries and inconsistencies of modern life (Now there's an idea for a television series!) but less so when it is directed at the offspring who are trying to help.

It can be personal:

'You never come to see me.'
'That's it. Leave me to struggle. Like you always do.'

It can have a wider target:

'Why has this happened to me? What have I done to end up like this? Someone up there has got it in for me.'

Always it is accusing and unpleasant.

4. *Denial*
One way of dealing with a problem is to pretend it isn't there. To ask for help is an admission of weakness, so let's go on as if everything is fine.

'I can do it myself.'
'I don't need the doctor.'
'The house doesn't need cleaning. We don't make any mess, just the two of us.'

Many a child of an elderly parent has viewed with dismay the chaos and disorder of the parent's living accommodation.

In the television situation comedy *Early Doors*, Joan and Eddy tell Tommy about the terrible state of Joan's elderly mother:

Joan:	She struggles getting upstairs so she sleeps in the chair…
Eddy:	Yeh, she sleeps in front of the telly. She can't get in and out of the bath so she doesn't bother...
Tommy:	How does she keep clean?
Eddy:	Well, she doesn't … just a quick all-over wash with a flannel in front of the kitchen sink on a morning – that's it.
Tommy:	It's a shame...
Eddy:	I say flannel … dishcloth really…

Extract from *Early Doors* by Craig Cash and Phil Mealey

5. Dependence

At the other end of the scale is dependence, – a total giving up any claim to autonomy which goes alongside an expectation that others (particularly the children, if they are at hand) will fill the gap, meeting physical, social and emotional needs.

This scenario is a cavernous hole which the most devoted son and daughter will never fill. Furthermore they will be continually dogged by a sense of failure. Their gaze meets the watery eyes of the aged parent and sees them ever hungry for more, more evidence of support, more news, more input of every kind. It will never be enough.

6. Stoicism

Some old people handle their increasing decrepitude with a touching stoicism. These are people who have imbibed the doctrine of atheistic evolution, whose cruel logic infers that a person's existence, after he has reproduced himself, is totally surplus to requirements. He has outlived his usefulness and must now live out his days causing as little trouble to everyone as possible. See the old man shuffle along with his frame and shopping bag, head bowed. Such people are trying to come to terms with the sad pointlessness of existence under that worldview. There is a quiet resignation about them. They put me in mind of a person who realises vaguely that he has left something important somewhere but he can't remember what or where.

7. Faith

But in contrast to stoicism there is the response of faith, which might look like stoicism but it has a smile on its face.

This song by a Christian singer/songwriter is the faith response to feebleness:

> Well my body gets so tired
> Living with these aches and pains.
> But I got myself a deal where it's gonna be exchanged.
> That's why I'm thankful and I'm grateful
> I've only got one life to live.
> When I die I'm going to heaven and I won't be back again.
>
> Yes, things always could be better
> But then again things could be worse.
> And I've got the greatest love in all the universe.
> My intention to be thankful
> Even when I'm old and grey.
> Want to leave this world of trouble with a smile upon my face.

Extract from *I'm grateful* by Bryn Haworth

Faith makes a difference because instead of seeing the road as being all downhill to the grave, it enjoys the prospect beyond the funeral. There really is something to look forward to – something big. This Christian hope is memorably expressed by C. S. Lewis at the close of his Narnia stories:

> 'The term is over: the holidays have begun. The dream is ended: this is the morning.'
>
> And as He spoke He no longer looked to them like a lion; but the things that began to happen after that were so great and beautiful that I cannot write them. And for us this is the end of all the stories, and we can most truly say that they all lived happily ever after. But for them it was only the beginning of the real story. All their life in this world and all their adventures in Narnia had only been the cover and the title page: now at last they were beginning Chapter One of the Great Story which no one on earth has read: which goes on forever: in which every chapter is better than the one before.

> Extract from *The Last Battle* by C. S. Lewis

Only a Biblical worldview can both understand ageing and provide a positive response. It is that of the apostle Paul in his second letter to the church at Corinth:

> Therefore we do not lose heart. Though outwardly we are wasting away, yet inwardly we are being renewed day by day. For our light and momentary troubles are achieving for us an eternal glory that far outweighs them all. So we fix our eyes not on what is seen but on what is unseen. For what is seen in temporary, but what is unseen is eternal.
>
> Now we know that if the earthly tent we live in is destroyed, we have a building from God, an eternal house in heaven, not built by human hands. Meanwhile we groan, longing to be clothed with our heavenly dwelling, because when we are clothed, we will not be found naked. For while we are in this tent we groan and are burdened,

because we do not wish to be unclothed but to be clothed with our heavenly dwelling, so that what is mortal may be swallowed up by life (2 Cor. 4:16–5:4).

So that is old age: beset by foolishness, feebleness, frustration and fear and overlaid by a mixture of a range of responses, some negative, some positive, some endearing, some infuriating.

When we are faced with an unattractive response we need to recall the underlying struggle.

Your aged parent may be a Christian believer. But the extract above reminds us that although there is plenty of scope for hope there is also room for gloom – there will be groaning; there are burdens. The trial of old age is immense and the response of faith may not be the first one you, the carer, see.

Your aged parent may not be a believer. He or she has ultimately nothing to look forward to. That is grim for them and almost as grim for you. But what a kind God it is who has allowed them to live this long, thus extending to them the day of grace and giving them time yet to repent and trust Jesus Christ.

In this chapter we have seen that it is hard to be old. None of us should underestimate the trials that are ahead of us.

5

WHAT HAVE I GOT TO GIVE?

*In which I offer a tool for
a needs assessment exercise.*

Two boy scouts were helping an old lady across the road.

> 'Why does it take two of you?' somebody asked.
> 'In case she doesn't want to go,' they replied.

It is entirely possible to give help which is inappropriate, even unwanted, as when a gentleman offers his seat on the tube to a feminist. The backlash is scary. The difference is that normally an old person has not had assertiveness training. But we must beware of doing things for our parents from a motive of needing to feel better about ourselves. Perhaps your Mother doesn't want to be invited for Christmas; perhaps she really means it when she says she is happy to be quiet in her own home by herself. Sometimes we just want to tick the box marked 'Mum and Dad' so that we feel free to then get on with other items on our agenda. And we don't hear or don't believe them when they try to say what they want or don't want.

It can be really offensive to an older person to be treated in this way.

All the rest of the day Angela watched Valerie with Mother and saw herself in every action. When Valerie carefully helped Mother to her unsteady feet – arm round her ample waist, legs braced in an exaggerated fashion to take her weight, face set in an expression of extreme concern – Angela saw how unbearable this solicitous behaviour was to Mother. It underlined Mother's difficulties. Everything Valerie did was a grotesque parody of what it should have been – all that was needed to get Mother up was the simple offer of a hand to pull on. There was in the inclination of Valerie's head as she bent towards Mother something offensive – it was as though Valerie was following stage directions of a crude and over-colourful variety. Nothing was spontaneous. Even Valerie's conversation smacked of condescension with its little set pieces topped and tailed for Mother's benefit.

Extract from *Mother can you hear me?* By Margaret Forster

Integral to treating ageing people with respect is the policy of listening to what they say and not riding roughshod over their dignity by insisting on doing for them what they can do for themselves or what they see as superfluous. To a hygiene conscious, tidy minded woman with good eyesight it can be tempting to march into an old person's chaos with the Marigolds on and the anti-bacterial spray at the ready. But that is to forget the person at the centre. How would you feel if someone did that to you in your home? Unless the situation is life-threatening, surely it is in keeping with respect and sensitivity to ignore the muddle and focus on the person. In my experience of many years of visiting elderly people, what they value most is your company and conversation. Offer your cleaning services but don't insist unless the want of hygiene is life-threatening.

So this chapter, to borrow social workers' jargon, is about putting together a package of care.

A. A realistic assessment

It is axiomatic that everyone is different. And that applies to old people: their needs are not identical. While some ninety year olds are wonderfully and fiercely capable and independent, others are utterly lost and helpless. So, when it comes to your parents, start by thinking about what it might be they are lacking for a comfortable old age. Consider the questions under the various categories of need. Under each heading I will list some practical ideas for solutions. Forgive the obvious nature of many. But sometimes the answer is simple and we just don't want to see it. The list, of course, is not exhaustive. Supplement it with your own ideas.

1. Social needs
Is it company they lack?
    Are they on their own, unable to get out?
    Do they spend days when they see nobody?

* Pop in – little and often is good.
* Take others with you to visit
* Take them out to see old friends and family
* Take them out to lunch
* Encourage them to specifically invite people to come round for coffee
* Organise regular transport to a day centre
* Take them to church and church events

- Arrange for or transport an old friend to visit them
- Encourage use of the telephone

2. Emotional needs

Are they feeling abandoned and left out?
Do they feel useless?
Do they think that no one cares?
Are they inclined to depression?
Are they hungry for news and a slice of life?

- Visit and take your coat off and have a cup of tea even if you don't feel like one.
- Listen to their troubles
- Take them seriously
- Sympathise
- Share news and details of your life
- Ask them for advice
- Involve them in discussion
- Listen to their comments and suggestions
- Frequently recall happy times
- Encourage them about the way they have helped and supported you
- Thank them
- Tell them you love them
- Joke and laugh
- Send them postcards
- Make a fuss of them on their birthday
- Include them in family events
- Telephone
- Enjoy chatting over common interests together (like football)
- Let them buy you things occasionally and be appreciative
- Hold their hands
- Hug them

3. Intellectual needs

Do they seem bored?

Do they not know how to fill their time?

Are they limited in their conversation?

- Talk to them about wide-ranging issues, not just about their health or their troubles.
- Encourage reading of the newspaper
- Save cuttings for them
- Lend books you have enjoyed and then discuss
- If their eyesight is poor, get hold of tapes, CDs
- Do the crossword together
- Encourage radio listening
- Introduce them to the wider choice of channels
- If they have the dexterity, get hold of a laptop and introduce them to the internet
- Take them to lectures, concerts, theatre
- Take them to church
- Play scrabble or chess
- Watch the TV with them and discuss the content

4. Practical needs

Do they have a problem with domestic chores?

Can they manage the garden?

How do they get from A to B?

Is their accommodation warm enough?

Can they do their own shopping and cooking?

Can they operate the washing machine?

Do they need and are they willing to move to more suitable accommodation?

- Offer to run the vacuum cleaner round
- Advertise for a cleaner
- Cut the grass

- Look out for a gardener
- Find out about the local bus or train service
- Recommend a friendly reliable taxi service
- At the beginning and end of British summer time offer to change the clocks, video and central heating control
- Take them shopping to stock up the freezer
- Recommend simple, easy to prepare menus
- Bring something to eat that is homemade and tasty
- Take away heavy items for washing
- Offer to do some ironing
- Offer to go with them to look at alternative properties

5. Personal needs

Can they dress themselves?
   Can they wash and keep clean?
   Can they move safely around the flat/house?
   Can they manage to get to the toilet?
   Can they feed themselves adequately?
   Can they cut manage shaving/ nail-cutting?
   Do they need to see a dentist/have a new denture?
   Are their feet in good shape?
   How do they get their hair cut/cared for?

- Get them to apply for Attendance Allowance
- Suggest they use it to buy in some help
- Investigate whether they are eligible for homecare from Social Services
- Arrange for someone to be there at the most vulnerable times
- Apply for some rails or other equipment to be fitted, via Social services
- Encourage them to invest in clothing/shoes which are easy to put on and remove

- Investigate local chiropodists/podiatrists
- Take to the dentist or find out about one who will visit
- Offer to cut their nails
- Take to suitable hairdresser
- Trim, wash and set hair

6. Financial/Organisational needs

Can they make ends meet?

Are they worrying about whether they have enough money?
Are their affairs in order?
Are they dealing with bills sensibly?
Are they able to access their money when they need to?
Do they know where their important documents are?
Have they made a will?

- Arrange for a financial adviser to call
- Be willing to be present when he/she does
- Arrange for power of attorney for yourself and a sibling
- Encourage direct debits for regular bills
- Offer to assist in sorting through ancient papers
- Suggest they make a will

7. Spiritual needs

Are they ready to die?

Do they face death with confidence in Christ?
Do they get opportunity to hear the gospel?
Do they pray?
Would they like to go to church?
Can they access a Bible?
- Pray for them
- Talk naturally to them about how the Lord encourages you in your life
- Pray with them

- Offer to read the Bible or a Christian book to them
- Sing hymns to/with them
- Arrange transport to a local church
- Encourage other Christians to visit and talk of spiritual things
- Bring appropriate Christian literature for them
- Speak about the reality of heaven
- Encourage them to pray for others

B. A realistic approach

If, when you have done the above assessment with one of your parents in mind, you find yourself overwhelmed and are thinking of emigrating, be calm and read on.

This chapter's heading is deliberately ambiguous: '**What have you got to give?**' has been all about trying to see what it is precisely your aged parent needs. It might be minimal or maximal, high maintenance or low maintenance. If you have accepted that your parents' welfare in their old age is your concern, that assessment is the place to start. And that assessment needs to be repeated from time to time as the ageing process takes its toll and needs change.

But it isn't the whole story. Ask the question another way: 'What have *you* got to give?' is about working out what you personally can realistically offer in this situation.

I fully accept that not everyone will be able to do what I did. There are other commitments, other pressures which limit the time that can be spent personally meeting your parents' needs. In some cases you just do not have the necessary expertise. Then there is distance. You might suggest your parents move nearer to you, but they might be unwilling to face such upheaval. You might consider moving nearer to them but that has huge implications for your work, family and church commitments.

One answer is delegation. This idea is built into some of the suggestions listed earlier in the chapter. Just as most of us do not educate our children ourselves but delegate that part of our parental responsibility to a school, so there are various agencies which undertake to provide for the diverse needs of the elderly. There are care homes, which is the ultimate delegation; there are agencies, social services, charities, neighbours, friends, siblings, other relatives, and churches.

There will always be some delegation, unless you have qualifications up to your armpit and no life of your own. But before you start thumbing the yellow pages, assess the needs according to the categories above and see what actually you could or should offer yourself. And read some of the preceding chapters again to remind yourself that your aged parent might rightly need to be moved up your list of priorities.

As to your own input: it can be occasional, regular or full-on.

1. Occasional

Occasional does not necessarily mean rare, but it does imply that the contact is less frequent and irregular. For some elderly parents input does not have to be routinely scheduled and they would be insulted if it were.

Rather the occasional input occurs when you make the most of being in the area and call in for an impromptu visit; it means using a spare half-hour to chat on the phone; it means paying attention to special events (anniversaries/ birthdays) to let your parents know how important they are to you.

The advantages of occasional input are:

- It is time-efficient at a busy time of life

- It is special
- It has the joy of spontaneity and surprise (even if you planned it)
- It is less likely to be tedious and therefore you can be genuinely enthusiastic
- You will have a lot of news to share because you are with them less often
- You make a big effort
- If it is unannounced you pre-empt expectation and subsequent disappointment

The disadvantages of occasional input are:

- In a busy life you might forget altogether and neglect your parents
- You cannot be depended on for helpful routine support
- You might not really know what is going on in terms of your parents' needs and comfort

2. Regular
Regular might mean input on a daily, weekly, monthly or even annual basis. It represents an agreed commitment to your parents to a certain level of contact, possibly to supply particular needs. It might work alongside the occasional extra (see above) or it might be a routine which suits your lifestyle and theirs. Examples are the phone call every morning at 8.15, an invitation to lunch every Sunday, the popping in to cut the grass once a fortnight or the toenails once a month.

Some advantages of regular input are:
- It is a comfortable routine
- You can set your input to a manageable level
- It ensures you do not totally neglect your parents

- It lends structure for your parents to a week/day/month
- It provides them with an 'event' to look forward to
- It inspires confidence that certain things are taken care of

Some disadvantages of regular input are:

- You might not be able to keep it up
- It sets up expectations
- If you don't, for example, telephone at 8.15, they worry
- It can get mechanical and boring
- It might blind you to other needs because you have 'ticked the boxes'

3. Full-on

Full-on is when you have become a primary carer, meeting a wide range of needs on a daily basis. It might mean a live-in situation or a turning up several times a day to perform tasks essential to existence.

Some advantages to full-on care are:

- You really do know what is going on
- You are in a position to pre-empt serious bother, allay anxiety or call in experts
- The aged parent is likely to be very well-cared for
- The aged parent is likely to feel very safe
- You get to know other people who service your parents
- Your presence ensures they get care of the highest standard

Some disadvantages to full-on care:

- You are tied
- You are in danger of becoming exhausted
- There may be unnecessary over-dependence

So what have you got to give? Only you can answer that question and you cannot answer it until you have faced the question of what is needed, and have looked at your own life.

The bundle of love

To talk about a package of care sounds very cold and clinical. I prefer to call it a bundle of love.

You might visit faithfully and frequently, you might buy expensive presents and pay for the very best in professional help, you might phone every day and give every Saturday to doing jobs for them in house and garden, but if you have not love ...

> Love is patient, love is kind. It does not envy, it does not boast, it is not proud. It is not rude, it is not self-seeking, it is not easily angered, it keeps no record of wrongs. Love does not delight in evil but rejoices with the truth. It always protects, always trusts, always hopes, always perseveres (1 Cor. 13:4-7).

6

NOBODY SAID IT WAS EASY

In which I examine the pitfalls of caring.

If you have ever made a resolution to do something, something that is right and good, something you really want to do in the service of people you love, but something which is going to invade your time on a frequent and regular basis, you will know that the enthusiasm can fade away pretty quickly when the reality sets in.

Someone said to me when I explained how I spent my days during the period of caring for my father-in-law – 'It's like a having a baby again'. And so it was, but minus the cuddles and chuckles and the smell of Johnson's baby powder on the peachy soft skin.

Consider this scenario and see if it rings any bells:

To answer the telephone on a Sunday afternoon and hear her Father's voice was alarming and meant disaster. She gave the number and he said, 'Is that you, Angela?' which irritated her. Who else could it be since her voice was that of an adult female and no other adult female lived in the house? In ways like that she was cruel to him.

'Yes, of course,' she said, curtly, though she had caught the despondency in his voice and interpreted it correctly with great speed. 'Is anything wrong?' Because she was a Trewick by birth, Angela knew that this was the expected thing to assume.

'It's your Mam.'

Naturally. It always was. Nothing else made the stomach lurch with such violence.

'What's happened?'

'She's took bad. I took her breakfast in, bran and that, got her up, got her dressed and nice, said she wouldn't bother with her hair but I said oh no we're not starting that game and I did it, best I could like, anyways I got her going and I thought hello her mouth's a bit funny but she says she's all right, bad tempered like, and anyways when I came from getting a loaf- I had to get a loaf or I wouldn't have left her – anyways she says she wants to lie down so I took off her slippers and she lay down on the settee, but her colour was bad mind' –

He had to be heard out. Even if she could have brought herself to, Angela would never have interrupted. She listened almost dreamily, absent minded, picking at a bit of fluff on her sleeve. Perhaps he would go on forever and nothing need be done.

– 'anyways she tries to get up to go to the doings and she was away, down in a flash, head missed the fender by an inch, like a log, couldn't move her and she's shaking and her face all screwed up – what a business – oh dear – so I grabbed the poker and banged on the wall for Mrs Collins and luckily she was in and got the message – anyways she came and between us we got her back on the settee – she's deadweight, you'd never think, till you come to lift her – and Mrs Collins says straight away "she's had a stroke, Mr Trewick" and by god he was damned right, the doctor said "she's had a stroke" soon as he'd seen her, and I must say he came quick, just a young fellow but very nice, "she's had a stroke" he says, but that was yesterday – what a night – and now this morning she's worse, a bit of pneumonia got into her the doctor says' –

'How awful,' Angela said. He had paused too long for breath for her to ignore the break. 'Poor Mother.'

'Poor Mother all right,' Father said, 'you're dead right there – thought she was a goner – but anyways I'm managing and we'll see how she goes – the doctor's coming back this afternoon and he's given her pills and everything, course she can't hardly swallow, can't speak either, it's a job getting anything into her but I'm managing and Mrs Collins is very good' –

'I'd better come down,' Angela said. There was no alternative. She despised herself for the grudging way in which she said it, but Father did that to her.

Extract from *Mother can you hear me?* By Margaret Forster

'Father did that to her.' What we do to others we never know. The best of relationships is tainted with sin. There is manipulation; there is suspicion of manipulation; there are messages spoken and unspoken, understood, resisted or misunderstood.

In this chapter we are going to look at some of the hazards of caring for the aged parent. We shall open a window on what might be going on in the mind of the person who wipes the dribble off Dad's chin. It is not a pretty sight and I am not talking about the dribble. As God said to Cain, 'Sin is crouching at your door: it desires to master you..'.

Now, I know there is pleasure in service; there is delight in making someone comfortable; it is truly better to give than to receive. I also know my own sinful heart and I think it is fair to assume that I am not the only sinner on the planet. In taking on the care of an elderly parent we need to keep an eye on our own emotional responses and deal with them, not deny them.

1. The five bad boys of caring

So here are the five bad boys of caring, running amok behind the closed door of your smiling face. If you are a carer and have never faced these beasts, you are farther along the sanctification road than I am. But watch out, they might be lurking yet and waiting to get you.

A. Anger

You can feel as if your life has been hi-jacked. You planned to read the newspaper/ watch Neighbours/ embroider a cushion/ make a casserole/ or just go to work and you get a phone-call.

You could have been winning the Nobel prize for literature but you are pushing a wheelchair.

The more you attempt to meet needs the more you perceive that the needs are endless. The loneliness of the old lady you visit is a gaping bottomless pit. It doesn't matter how long you stay, when you get up to go she says:

'Are you going already?'

And then comes the accusatory comment:

'I know you're very busy.'

Followed by the twist of the knife:

'I'm such a nuisance to everybody.'

And inside you feel a kind of rage, that nothing would be enough. It is not gratitude you want, although appreciation is nice. Possibly you crave the recognition by your parent that what they are asking is huge and that actually you had no choice. And your head is full of furious little speeches; now and then you rant to your friends about how unreasonable it all is. You make promises to yourself that you will not do this to your own children, promises which you are unlikely to keep.

But beyond that, the anger is directed not at your parent but at God. You feel that he has stitched you up and prevented you from following your own agenda. And you mourn the loss of the life you might have had.

B. Being a martyr

So you suppose you had better do it. It's ghastly and tedious and miserable but someone's got to do it and as usual, the finger is pointing at you. Deep, deep sighs. It is Saturday afternoon and you are watching a football match on television when the phone rings. Pulling a face lined with premonition, you pick up the phone. Your family hear your end of the conversation which goes something like this:

'What is it you want?'

'You want me to come round?'

'I'll come round now.'

'I was watching the football, but it's OK I'll come round now.'

'No, don't phone Mary. I'll do it. It's got to be done. It better be done now. Give me five minutes.'

'No. I'm coming. I'll be there. Just give me five, OK?'

The receiver is replaced. Lips are set tight as you reach for your coat, shout goodbye and doggedly make your way.

You are fed up about missing the football (but secretly not as much as you first thought because England were losing and it wasn't that good) and now you are hugging the idea that you are better than Mary because you are dealing with this at an observable cost to yourself. Already you are rehearsing the story for your friends and you emerge the noble hero.

> 'I had *just* sat down to watch the football, cup of tea in my hand…'

You are proud of your sacrifice and enjoying the right to be angry with just about everybody, because you had to do it and no one else offered.

C. Control

The fact is, to continue the story of the interrupted football game, you didn't want anyone else to offer; you made sure no one else had the chance to offer. This is because you are going for superhero status. You think if I take this on I am going to be brilliant at it. People will be impressed at my superb self-sacrifice (memo to myself – must slip it into the conversation).

Now in order to be that good you have to be very controlling. You control who else is busy around your parents. It looks like a demonstration of your concern for their welfare, but actually it is not about them it is about you. You fear lest others should be seen as more helpful to your parents than you are. You are jealous lest others rise in their affections or are seen as more dependable. You hate being indispensable but you also love it and don't want to share that no 1 slot with anyone. You want to be the one they need for their comfort in old age. Perhaps you fear they'll leave all their money to the cleaner.

This feeling of your importance to the whole set-up is your pay-off for all you have given, which has been genuine and well intentioned. How the human heart, since Eden, craves glory, if not of one kind, then another.

D. Drudgery

Some levels of care, especially the daily variety, can be mind-numbingly tedious. The washing and the dressing and the servicing of physical needs are repeated so often that you can do them on automatic pilot. You clear up a mess and next time you arrive, there it is again. It can be depressing to do the same menial task so often and to consider that this now makes up your life – the days stretching out like an American interstate, mile on dreary mile towards the distant horizon. You start reading the death columns in the newspaper and note with alarm that most deaths seem to occur when people are in their nineties. You do the maths. How long can you sustain what you do? And of course the prospect is only for further degeneration and decrepitude, yours and your parent's.

Even the weekly visit or phone-call can be very tedious, especially if there is any dementia or particular obsessions. The same conversations are rehearsed:

'Did you see Carol Vordermann's dress on Countdown?'
'No, I don't watch Countdown. I'm at work.'
'She wears the most peculiar outfits.'

You sit and listen stroking a hand, and smile and make sympathetic noises, staring into the middle distance, trying to think of a change of subject. You surreptitiously glance at the clock and wonder when you can decently make a move. You are bored and you fear it shows.

E. Exhaustion

You have set yourself a heady pace and it is taking its toll. Helping Dad out of his chair is physically exhausting – he's a big man and his legs do not take his weight. You are rushing from A to B, squeezing in a visit between going to the dump and collecting your daughter from orchestra practise. You are being asked a lot of questions. You are trying to work out who will get Mum to the dentist and what will happen when you go on holiday. Every bone in your body aches and you are close to tears a lot of the time.

Mentally and physically you are exhausted and you do not respond well to the comment by your mother that you look tired and her well-intentioned question:

'Are you sure you are not overdoing it?'

2. Why those bad boys must be faced

The writer of the letter to the Hebrews includes this stirring injunction:

Make every effort to live in peace with all men and to be holy; without holiness no one will see the Lord. See to it that no-one misses the grace of God and that no bitter root grows up to cause trouble and defile many (Heb. 12:14-15).

The expressions 'make every effort' and 'see to it' tell us that a struggle is involved here. It is much easier to be cross with everybody than to live at peace with them.

Relationships of all kinds challenge us at the very heart of our sinful nature; they expose our basic tendency to be selfish. We will never be perfectly holy, but holiness should be our aim. And if we are not bothered about holiness, then it is likely that we don't know Christ at all, because he is bothered about it – that is why he gave his life.

The thing about those five bad boys, anger, being a martyr, control, drudgery and exhaustion, is that they are great pals and when they get together they cause trouble. They are not all sinful in themselves – it is not a sin to be tired nor to find certain tasks tedious – but when exhaustion and drudgery join forces with the others they become demolition partners. Here are some things they demolish:

- Goodwill – what you started out of a heart to honour your parents and Christ has now become cold duty which can, unchecked, turn love to hatred.

- Peace of mind – when we choose anger or being a martyr and carry that spirit around in us as we tend to our elderly parents, the Holy Spirit is grieved and Satan is given a foothold. We rightly feel troubled.

- Joy in service – God loves a cheerful giver and it is a joyous and liberating thing to give (money, time or energy) out of a full heart of thankfulness to God. There is massive happiness in this, which those who serve self or money would never believe. But when we are grudging and resentful, all of that joy evaporates.

- Relationship with God – our own horror at how much time we are spending on our parents has inflated ourselves and our importance. God has diminished to the very edge of the picture – even perhaps out of it altogether – and ourselves and our needs are right in the centre. This is a very unhealthy place to be.

And here are the weapons of mass destruction that the bad boys, working together, manufacture:

- Bad temper – we are on a short fuse and respond to simple and harmless requests with irritation, which will show. My father-in-law suffered with itching, the source of which no consultant could ever identify, and his frequent plaintiff request to anybody passing his chair was, 'Rub my back, will you.' I rubbed his back all right, but there was sometimes a complete lack of tenderness in the ointment. It was somewhat fortunate that the harder I rubbed the better he liked it.

- Violence – it is now well documented that old people are often physically abused, even by their offspring. We might all think we would never do that, but put those bad boys together and it could happen one day. A nice Christian believer like you could one day be driven over the edge to do the unthinkable.

- Walking out –. Yes, weariness in well-doing can lead to such massive discouragement, with yourself as much as anything, that you give up altogether. You get your bag: 'That's it; I'm off'. What pain that can cause to your vulnerable parents. What guilt you will carry. How will that relationship be restored?

- Bitterness – the verses in Hebrews 12 warn us about the root of bitterness. This is a most pernicious plant, sown by the seed of unchecked anger. We look around us and see others having, apparently, an easy ride. And we hate them for it. We consider that we have been dealt a dreadful hand and we think we deserved better. We are cynical about people, even when they try to help. We impute the very worst of motives to them. We imitate a hedgehog for prickliness and untouchableness and then blame those who leave us alone, even though we have encouraged them to do it.

- Blaming – ever since the Garden of Eden human beings have looked round for someone to blame. On my bad days, I blamed my father-in-law, my mother-in-law, my husband, and of course God himself. And in every case the relationship was soured. Not only so, but I was self-righteously telling myself lies, and believing them. When we murmur at God's wise decrees or distrust his providence in this way we are dethroning God, and guess who the usurper is!

Do you see now why anger, being a martyr, control, drudgery and exhaustion must be faced squarely and dealt with? They are extremely dangerous. Do not deny their existence and let them continue their work, like undetected terrorists making bombs in a terraced house in Wapping. Send in the armed response unit!

3. How to handle those bad boys

Practical strategies I will suggest in the next chapter. But there is a much deeper response and it has to do with the way we think. When the apostle Paul says in Romans 12 'be transformed by the renewing of your mind' he is not encouraging us all to study with the Open University. Rather he is underlining the truth that it is the way we think about things which truly will shape our behaviour. Christian doctrine is not to be shut up in dusty tomes in the Bodleian Library and only referred to by learned academics – it is absolutely crucial for every believer in Jesus Christ to understand the truth about God, his character and work. Otherwise we cannot understand or relate properly to the world we live in. Renewing our minds by filling them with the truth about God and about ourselves will have a transforming effect on the way we live.

So here follows the briefest of resumes of aspects of the character of God which will, if served up and ingested regularly, beat those bad boys out of sight. For a fuller treatment I recommend, seriously, an intake of Jim Packer, Wayne Grudem, John Calvin or any of the puritans.

- God is sovereign. He is sovereign over the whole universe. He created it and he sustains it. He is intimately connected with it and he directs all the affairs of men. Nothing happens in the world without his permission. That includes you and me, our parentage, our location and situation today and every day. Relax – you are not general manager of the universe. The universe is in much safer, wiser and more capable hands than yours (Dan. 4:35; Rom. 11:33-36).

- God is good. The goodness of God is enough to make you weep. Every day the sun rises and you have light and warmth. You have breath and energy. You have food and clothing. And this is what God does for millions upon millions of humankind who never give him a first thought, let alone a second one. Not only so, but as God writes human history he does so with a good end in view. He is not like those malicious gods of ancient Greece who just played around with human kind, taunting them and wasting them for fun, rendering their lives pointless. He has planned and executed the redemption of humanity from the mess they have wilfully and rebelliously created for themselves. This good purpose includes you if you have put your trust in the one God sent to achieve this redemption, Jesus Christ. Now having gone to all that trouble to rescue you, God is not now callously going to abandon you to a series of random and painful events to upset you. In *his* goodness he has planned for *your* goodness. That process might involve some pain, – is anything of value achieved without pain? – but the pain and difficulty comes from the hand of a loving God. And the pain and difficulty is temporary; the best of happy endings awaits and it is permanent (Gen. 50:20; Rom. 8:28-32).

• God is all-powerful. God is the one who can. He makes things happen; he reverses outcomes; he delights to do the impossible. Frequently it pleases him to do this kind of thing in answer to the humble requests of his beloved children. His power raised Jesus Christ from the dead; his power caused us to reach out to Jesus for rescue; that same power is a resource available to his people so that in weakness they find that they have strength (Luke 1:37; Eph. 1:19-20; Ps. 121:2).

• God knows. He knows what you did today and he knows what you will face tomorrow. He knows about your tears and sighs and struggles and sins. If blame is to be apportioned, he will do it justly and at the right time. He knows your frame and your frailty. He never sleeps so that you can sleep in safety (Pss. 139:1-3; 121:3-4; 103:13-14).

• God is gracious. His love for humans is an unrequited love, demonstrated in the sending of his Son. He gives us what we don't deserve – forgiveness and the assurance of a home in heaven. This immense gift is free (although it cost him a lot) and available to recalcitrant rebels, offensive offenders (Rom. 5:8; Eph. 2:1-5; 2 Tim. 1:9).

Please forgive the shortness of that summary. One could go on and on and I was tempted to. But the point I want to make is that even a minor meditation on the character of God will impact the responses I have described as bad boys in this chapter. They will start to shrivel and slink away in shame. How can self-importance be sustained when we think about the greatness of God? He is the centre, not me. How can we be angry when we consider the goodness and the grace of God? If we start getting on our high horse and ranting about what we deserve, won't we dismount and shut up when we recall that what we actually deserve is something a lot worse than cleaning up pooh from a carpet? How can we keep up a stupid martyr act when we remember that God sees and knows all things? How can we grasp for control and glory when we recall that God is king and the glory is his? Even drudgery is lifted when we make it our goal to please him. And exhaustion is reduced when we appreciate that God is not a cruel taskmaster. He not only permits, he commands regular rest. He also promises strength for each day and is able to supply it.

There may be some repenting to be done over ungodly and resentful attitude. But God is an extraordinarily forgiving God. He is the Father who watches the road for the sight of his returning wayward son and runs to meet him. There is truly no-one like Almighty God.

> 'Who is a God like you, who pardons sin and forgives the transgression of the remnant of his inheritance?' (Micah 7:18).

It is undeniably true that the person who cares for an elderly parent may frequently suffer at the hands of an ungrateful, grumpy or manipulative old man or woman. It happens; it is the kind of thing that people do to each other. But the recipient of God's free pardon for a debt of sin he or she could never pay, is in a good position to forgive the ill-humours of old age. Indeed Jesus reminded Peter (Matt. 18:21-35) that there is really no comparison between the abuse God has suffered at our hands and the abuse we might suffer from a fellow sinner. And yet God has let us off. We are thus required to do the same. No ifs, no buts, and as often as necessary.

> Bear with each other and forgive whatever grievances you may have against another. Forgive as the Lord forgave you (Col. 3:13).

7

How to care for your aged parent and stay sane

In which I suggest some practical strategies.

There are dozens of different and satisfactory ways of caring for elderly parents. But most of them will be difficult to maintain at times. However willing you are to take it on, some practical strategies will help you to fulfil your commitment, which, let's face it, is of indeterminable length.

This chapter outlines the kind of strategies which I found helpful. The list is not exhaustive, of course. For a book which details all kinds of practical help, ideas and useful resources and contacts, I recommend *The Daily Telegraph* guide:'A survival guide to later life' by Marion Shoard.

My own personal list, based on my experience, falls into two clusters: there are strategies which relate to your input and there are strategies which relate to your sanity. I found I needed both.

A. Managing the load

People who in the course of their work have to bear heavy loads are trained in technique. Health professionals are obliged to go on manual handling courses with tedious regularity. I was frequently reminded by those who cared for my father-in-law alongside me to keep a straight back, bend the knees, stand with feet apart, etc. etc. It was all in the interests of my health, safety and ability to continue doing the job. There are techniques you can learn to enable you physically to manage the load without wrecking your body. There are also resources you can acquire which make the job easier

But the offspring of a frail elderly parent need further techniques and resources to enable them to meet the emotional and time-consuming demands of the job. Here are five of the most useful.

1. Delegation

There are agencies which supply staff. If your parent is not eligible for help from social services, the social services office will supply you with a list of private care agencies. They also will provide on request a brochure containing details of all the approved residential care homes in your area, if you decide that is necessary.

Whatever the level of care need, there are, in theory at least, people who will supply that need, at a cost of course. And sometimes by taking that route you hit upon a person who is worth her weight in gold. If you find such a one, keep her on. Care workers are scandalously underpaid. Frequently they are women with children to provide for and they are usually hard up and interested in any extra work you can give them. Once your parent has got to know and like such a person, it makes sense to buy them in for little jobs that you can't manage yourself or to cover your time on holiday or a day off.

It should be pointed out here that care workers who are supplied by an agency are likely to be prohibited by the terms of their contract from freelancing in the way I am suggesting here. But it is an avenue worth exploring.

These workers if they become regular visitors to the household bring a good distraction to Mum or Dad; they bring a lively new window on the world, with their stories of their kids, their cat, their neighbours and their nights out. It is something very much to be encouraged, where it lightens your load to a more manageable level.

Keep on the look out for reliable and pleasant people who for a small fee will cut the grass, clean the flat, or take a parent to the doctors. You might meet some resistance from your parent and there might be financial constraints. Or not. Older people sometimes get out of touch with the cost of living and are ludicrously outraged at having to pay, say, £5 for a short taxi ride. They are perfectly comfortably off but they resent forking out. They expect you to rearrange your day so that you can run them to the doctors; they think because it costs them nothing, it costs you nothing. That is a tricky one and sometimes it is easier just to go along with it.

But the principle of delegation, in areas where it can be reasonably, usefully and acceptably applied is a good one. It releases you to maximise your input in other areas.

2. Inclusion

Of course you can delegate to your friends, if they are willing. You may get generous offers from people who volunteer to help now and then by giving you a night off.

I prefer to call that 'inclusion'. The Bible encourages us to carry each other's burdens and this is one way in which we can do it. Churches have a massive amount to offer in the care of old people: they have the motivation, the example, the encouragement, the command and the love. They have or should have a shared life, whereby we all know about and are concerned for each other's struggles and concerned to help where we can. Where most geographical communities in this country are merely notional and have no genuine commonality, a church is a genuine community with a common goal. They also are generally a mixed bunch of people with an extensive pool of talents, experiences and skills.

Small churches sometimes contain an overwhelming majority of older people. In such cases one could observe that there are not enough able-bodied people to minister to the older members in the ways I have been suggesting. But let us not ignore the fact that elderly people can help each other and should be encouraged to do so. Although most will suffer some decline in faculties with increasing age, their limitations are diverse and they can use their strengths to supply the weaknesses of others and vice versa.

The church supplied me with 'Charlie's Angels', – a group of Christian women who volunteered their support for me when I got involved in the care of my father-in-law after his discharge from hospital. Their commitment was staggering – these ordinary busy housewives/ workers who all had either salaried employment or young families or both. Yet they gave at least one afternoon a week for fifteen months to help me look after my father-in-law in his home. They did this with tenderness and compassion for my parents-in-law. They were and are true friends to me. More than that, these ordinary Christians were a shining testimony to Jesus Christ, for whose sake they gladly gave their time and their love. The health professionals who were involved in meeting my father-in-law's manifold health needs were staggered at the level of care and attention he received from these supposed amateurs. They many times separately acknowledged that they had never seen anything like it.

The inclusion of others made my work not only possible but more pleasant. On the most difficult days, it was helpful to have someone to share the more ghastly aspects of the work. Two are better than one in such circumstances. (See Eccles. 4:9, 10.) Apart from halving the work these excellent women instilled a sense of teamwork and camaraderie, not to mention a sense of humour. They were a continual fund of good sense and sound advice.

Whatever the level of care, it is good to include others in it, even occasionally. Other members of your family as well as good friends will help in a visit to your parents to keep the conversation going and provide distraction. Sometimes they turn out to be extremely knowledgeable in areas like setting the video (a 6 year old child), finding the stopcock (DIY enthusiasts) or haemorrhoids (retired district nurses).

3. The pre-emptive strike
Rather than waiting to be asked, which will probably occur at a time which is least convenient to you, why not get in first with a pre-emptive strike. Make regular offers to fetch something from the shops at a time when you yourself are going. Call in unexpectedly when you are passing for a short chat. People who live alone sometimes just want an opportunity to talk to someone for ten minutes or so a day. By offering that listening ear briefly but frequently, larger troubles and anxieties may be allayed.

And the carer breathes and sleeps more easily knowing that everything is ticking over as it should.

4. Routines

Older people, especially those who live alone, like their routines. I used to wonder why an old lady I visited got up so early every morning when the days were so long and time was so heavy on her hands. I wondered why she did not stay under the duvet an extra hour, as I would have liked to have done. What after all was the hurry? What did she have to get up for?

I do not recall whether I was foolish enough to voice those questions. Because the fact is that these routines that this lady had were what gave her days any purpose at all.

As a carer it can be helpful to slot into these routines. It could be taking Mum to have her hair done once a week or giving Dad a shave every other day. It makes for a short but purposeful contact, which is helpful and manageable on both sides.

If you are a daily visitor, it is helpful to set up routines which promote a healthy balance of rest and activity for your parents. It also prevents important things, like the taking of tablets for example, from being forgotten. So the day passes happily from the getting up and washing, through the drinking of coffee and the reading of the paper to the afternoon rest followed by the watch of Countdown. Somewhere amongst this daily/weekly programme you have laid down the boundaries and purpose of your own visit from the start and everyone knows what to expect. There is no argument, no uncertainty and no disappointment about what you did and the length of time you stayed.

5. Preparation

A nurse I know always goes into work with an interesting fact of the day to share with her patients. It is something distracting to talk about while she is giving injections or enemas.

People who are shut in their own homes are subject to the shrinking world syndrome. Their own troubles and concerns loom so large they eclipse more or less everything. So a diverting fact is like flinging open a window and letting in some good fresh air.

Sometimes I have visited with a number of family members or friends. If you are making a visit mob-handed it is quite a good idea to suggest that every member of the party has at least two topics for conversation. It might be an item of family news or the state of rainforest; it can be funny or informative, historic or contemporary; whatever it is, this kind of preparation pays big dividends. It prevents the tedium of repetition or silence. For your parents it is exciting and new, involving them in the wider world from which they so often feel their age excludes them.

Now that my own children have left home, I understand this hunger for a little window into the lives of one's children. It is not nosiness nor a desire to interfere, just a longing for a glimpse of some of the action.

'Have you got a lot to do today?' asked my mother-in-law as I put my coat on to leave.

I hesitated, wondering if this was a loaded question. Was she hoping I had time to do something else for her? I did not know quite how to answer. I always have plenty to do. I don't like idleness and I plan to be occupied every day.

'Oh, you know, a bit of this and a bit of that,' I finally answered non-committally.

I now realise that all my mother-in-law wanted to hear about was the busy trivialities of a normal domestic life.

She would have liked me to tell her that I was preparing a casserole of chicken, carrots and dumplings, or that I was checking out the charity shops for a blue t-shirt to go with my suit, or that I was changing the beds ready for the visit of my old school-friends, or preparing a Sunday school lesson on the prophet Micah. Anything really. Just a glimpse. Just that desire not to be completely out of everything that is going on out there.

We are not all natural chatterers. Some of us prefer conversation that moves in a straight line and sticks precisely to the point. The need-to-know basis is a general rule my children have used when speaking to me on the phone. And I have longed for the filling in of some of the irrelevant detail. So now I know how it feels.

Preparation for some conversational scenic routes makes a visit go so much better. Who knows where you will end up? You might catch yourself having a good time.

B Keeping your sanity
All of the above will help to lighten the load; they may also help to keep you cheerful or at least keep you going. This second cluster of strategies are designed to enhance the well-being of the carer, regardless of the feelings of the aged parent.

1. Submission
This takes us back to the synopsis of the doctrine of God in the previous chapter. This is the key not only to godliness but to the handling of any of the adverse circumstances we meet. Because God is who he is, because he has done for us what he has done, we can be delivered from the destructive power of adverse circumstances and negative emotions. There is always a 'but not'.

> We are hard pressed on every side but not crushed; perplexed but not in despair; persecuted but not abandoned; struck down but not destroyed (2 Cor. 4:8).

Now there is no comparison between even heavy duty care of an aged parent and the kind of thing the apostle Paul suffered as he preached the gospel of Christ, but the principle is the same for every believer. There is always a 'but not' in the most trivial domestic struggle. And that 'but not' stems from the knowledge of the power, wisdom and love of Almighty God, our heavenly Father. When facing the most apparently adverse providence, we can know that God has sent it and he is for us. So the answer is not to rant and rail but to submit.

There is a cut-through for pedestrians between our house and the flat where my parents-in-law lived. I called it sacrifice alley. Because as I walked it with monotonous regularity and wondered what I would find when I got to the flat, I could frequently have been heard repeating to myself these words:

> Therefore, I urge you, brothers, in view of God's mercy, to offer your bodies as living sacrifices, holy and pleasing to God – this is your spiritual act of worship (Rom. 12:1).

To meditate on God's mercy fits a person perfectly for the humblest service. To grasp the essence of true worship releases a person to gladly use hands, feet, face and voice not to please himself but to help others. I relish the moments when we strike up a great hymn of praise to God in the congregation on a Sunday morning. It is equally possible to relish the opportunity to give yourself, in particular your hands, in the most menial service because it has the same object, the glory of the Lord Jesus Christ. This is worship. And he is worthy.

A daily offering of yourself and all your faculties to God will keep you steady if not always ecstatic. You are liberated from seeking approval and appreciation from those for whom you care, because in a very real sense, you do not do it for them; you do it for Jesus.

And the perspective you receive from such meditation is that God supplies your needs on a daily basis, one day at a time. When I woke up each morning, I looked at the difficult day ahead and brought it before God in prayer.

'Can I do today?' I asked him.
And the answer was always, 'Yes, you can do today.'

And he was right. With his help I could.

2. Diversion

God has made us people with bodies, intellectual capacity, imagination, five senses, aptitudes and talents, a need for companionship and a sense of humour. We do not honour God when we become drudges. It is important and right to lead a balanced life, wherein we have time to develop our talents and appreciate the world God has made. King Solomon had a huge kingdom to rule and worldwide fame. Somehow in a busy life he pursued, for sheer pleasure I assume, a serious study of nature.

He described plant life, from the cedar of Lebanon to the hyssop that grows out of the walls. He also taught about animals and birds, reptiles and fish (1 Kings 4:33).

This same wise man wrote:

'A cheerful heart is good medicine, but a crushed spirit dries up the bones.'

So it is important, particularly if you are involved in heavy duty, full-on caring to get a life. Plan to do interesting things, things to stimulate your mind, exercise your body, stretch your imagination or just make you laugh. Do not neglect your friends.

Perfume and incense bring joy to the heart, and the pleasantness of one's friend springs from his earnest counsel (Prov. 27:9).

3. Respite

Respite can mean a friend undertaking to call in on your parent while you have a holiday, so that you can go away and not even make a phone call. Which is, by the way, a very good idea. Respite can also mean arranging for your parent to go into residential care for a week, whether you are away or not, *just so that you can have a break.*

I emphasise that last clause because it is sometimes very difficult to get an older person to agree to go into respite care. They may perceive themselves as getting less satisfactory care and attention; they may fear what is strange to them.

You have to repeat over and over again that respite care is not for their benefit but for yours, so that you will be able to continue offering the care that you do. You may be accused of being selfish, but do not let that deter you. It is part of being a responsible human being to consider the needs of others and there is every good reason for a cared for person to just occasionally consider the needs of the carer. Sometimes older people bemoan the fact that they cannot reciprocate; they might want to buy you chocolates or wine. But this is something they *can* do for you. If your care input is big and frequent and occasionally harrowing, it is a comfort to know that a break is coming up. And that break will restore you if you put aside false guilt and exercise faith that God can take care of the beloved parent. You are not indispensable.

Jesus himself saw the value and necessity of respite:

> Then, because so many people were coming and going that they did not even have a chance to eat, he said to them, 'Come with me by yourselves to a quiet place and get some rest' (Mark 6:31).

4. Creativity

By exercising the imagination it may be possible to inject some fresh air into whatever care you offer and prevent it becoming tedious and depressing.

The person you care for may be outwardly seriously disabled or extremely decrepit. However, inside there may be a young and lively mind which will appreciate being treated as a normal member of the human race. This was a point well made by the film 'Inside I'm dancing' in which two disabled young men were determined not to be put in a corner. They fought to have a slice of life and were not embarrassed to be out and about engaging in activities alongside others.

So take your blind friend for a feely shopping trip, trying out hats or sitting on sofas, just so that she can enjoy the sensation.

Find out about sports fixtures which might interest your Dad.

Invite your Mum to the children's activity at church where she can help by cutting out stuff for the craft or just by watching the door.

One day my father-in-law was very low. His head was down, he was hardly speaking. As I rubbed cream into his back I recalled a hymn we had sung that morning in church. So to the rhythm of my rubbing I struck up with Bunyan's classic 'Who would true valour see'. As I continued I heard this strange gravelly noise and I realised to my great delight that he recognised the hymn and was attempting to join in. He knew nearly all the words. After that I always sang to him while rubbing his back and it added a new and pleasurable dimension to my work as, en route to every visit, I selected the hymn. I discovered it was best to confine the repertoire to old school hymns as these were the ones he remembered best. We were both encouraged by the repetition of those fine words and stirring tunes.

This is but one example of how a little bit of creativity can turn tedium to pleasure for both yourself and the aged parent.

In Dickens' *Great Expectations* Wemmick has a delightful routine of firing a gun from his strange fort-like cottage every evening at precisely nine o'clock. It is a procedure which involves the Aged in heating up a poker until it is red-hot. Wemmick insists that 'it's the Aged's treat' but Pip is sure that it gives pleasure to Wemmick himself.

Drudgery can be diluted or even reversed. King Lear fondly hopes of a happy co-existence with his daughter Cordelia:

> So we'll live
> And pray, and sing, and tell old tales, and laugh
> At gilded butterflies.
> > Extract from *King Lear* by William Shakespeare

And why not?

5. Accountability

> A friend loves at all times, and a brother is born for adversity (Prov. 17:17).

Whenever we take anything on it is great to talk it over with a friend. When that project turns out to be a tough assignment, making huge emotional and physical demands, we will find great relief in talking it through with a Christian brother or sister. Such a friend will pray with you, restore your sense of perspective and sense of humour and challenge you if your attitude or behaviour is unworthy.

It is not merely sympathy you need; you also need someone who will recognise that the real struggle is with your emotional response to the situation and who will not be afraid to hold you to account for progress or otherwise towards godliness. Such a person will prevent you getting puffed up in your martyr spirit and will remind you of your resources in Christ. He or she will also tell you when you are driving yourself too hard and must slow down before you go bang.

Seek such a friend and encourage your friend to tell you the truth.

> Wounds from a friend can be trusted, but an enemy multiplies kisses (Prov. 27:6).

There is a very real danger of becoming weary in well-doing. That is why the apostle Paul wrote these words:

> Do not be deceived: God cannot be mocked. A man reaps what he sows. The one who sows to please his sinful nature, from that nature will reap destruction; the one who sows to please the Spirit, from the Spirit will reap eternal life. Let

us not become weary in doing good, for at the proper time we will reap a harvest if we do not give up. Therefore, as we have opportunity, let us do good to all people, especially to those who belong to the family of believers (Gal. 6:7-10).

To actively honour your mother or father is to sow to the Spirit. But the rewards might not be obvious and we might be tempted to give up. However the apostle reminds us that there will be a harvest, so this is most certainly a worthwhile thing to do. Christian believers can and should help each other to do good and continue to do good, by their prayerful and practical support.

8

IF IT'S NOT TOO MUCH TROUBLE

In which I suggest that the needs of the elderly present not just a challenge but an opportunity

Here is a typical conversation one might have with an older person:

You: Would you like to come to lunch on Sunday?
OP: If it's not too much trouble.
You: It's no trouble. Would you like to come?
OP: I don't want to be in your way.

Sometimes I have been sorely irritated by this kind of response. Of course, in one sense, it is more trouble to peel six potatoes instead of four. To offer hospitality to anyone is going to incur some sort of trouble of that kind. Presumably one knows that when one issues invitations and one is ready to tackle the extra work.

When receiving an invitation to lunch, the only appropriate response would seem to be either a 'Yes please' or a 'No thank you'. But instead every time we must go through this little self-deprecating rigmarole. There is, amongst the elderly, a craving for reassurance which must be satisfied. Rule No. 1 of the Old People's Charter must be obeyed: Thou shalt not put anyone out.

Sadly, old people can be so put down and disregarded by the world at large, that they might genuinely find it hard to believe that anyone would want them for their own sake or find pleasure in serving them.

One old lady I know will not accept a lift anywhere until she is convinced that the driver will be passing her door anyway. She will not take him out of his way. And she checks on a road map.

But why should we not put ourselves out for others?

And why should others not put themselves out for us?

Is it healthy to be totally self-sufficient, even if that were possible?

Isn't it helpful to be dragged from our natural inclination to total selfishness by being asked to attend to the needs of others?

Why can we not recognise that helping is part of the image of God in which we are made and therefore we will be happier if we do plenty of it?

Equally we all need to embrace the humility of accepting service from others, in allowing them to put themselves out for us, for this is the pattern the Master set.

To help someone, anyone, is by definition to go out of your way, to put yourself out. In one sense it is most definitely too much trouble, but that doesn't mean we shouldn't do it. Quite the reverse!

We read of the patriarch, Jacob, that he 'served seven years to get Rachel, but they seemed like only a few days to him because of his love for her.' But for most of us, who are not swept off our feet in the hot passion of romantic attachment, while love will lighten a heavy load it will not remove it. Some people serve seven years or more in affectionate attention to the needs and comfort of their parents in their old age. It is what they want to do; they know it is right to do it; but it is a huge burden.

I must tell the truth: I cared for my father-in-law for only fifteen months and sometimes the trouble seemed way too much; it was massive.

I was not an exemplary carer. But I learned some precious, vital and painful lessons for which I am very grateful. I thank God that he allowed me this experience; I would not have missed it for anything. I thank God for his grace, which renders the impossible possible, the unbearable bearable and the weak strong.

Putting yourself out for people is also an evidence of love. Isn't that what that Milk Tray advert was all about – the man who abseils down cliffs and crosses rivers in torrent to fetch a box of chocolates, all because the lady loves Milk Tray?

> 'We don't like to think of you travelling all that way in wintry conditions and on busy roads, just to spend a couple of hours with us.'

What can one answer? Only that, to borrow the L'Oreal catchphrase, 'You are worth it.'

The future's grey

The bulging post-war baby boom generation is about to hit retirement age. There will be in the next thirty years, unless Jesus Christ returns, an even greater proportion of the population receiving their bus passes. Many of this generation will live to their nineties with varying and increasing degrees of frailty.

So the challenge of the aged parent will not diminish. The discussion about euthanasia, voluntary or otherwise, will not go away.

Those who know the value God places on every human life must be ready to put their money where their mouth is. If we believe that every crumbling human frame houses a precious living soul, how will we demonstrate that value to a cynical, hard-hearted world? The answer is that we must personally roll up our sleeves and get involved.

The challenge is individual, to the offspring of surviving parents.

The challenge is also to the church. This challenge is also a tremendous opportunity.

While the National Health Service is apparently in terminal failure, dying for want of resources, sensible management and a coherent philosophy of care and service, churches have a real opportunity to show what care in the community can be. Bring on the Christians.

Too often evangelical churches have focused effort and attention on the young to the neglect of those teetering on the brink of eternity. Sometimes our works of mercy have been concentrated on headline-catching needs and we have been blind to those everyday needs of ageing people in our streets or even in our pews.

But every congregation of believers in Jesus Christ can demonstrate the grace of God in action by its treatment of and attention to the elderly. This is gospel work. By means of a team effort, which harnesses its collective skills and resources, local churches could make a difference and make an impact for Christ. Small churches might be able to work together and pool resources and personnel to create teams. Such teams could help a church member bear the burden of care for a frail parent; they could ameliorate the life of this and that old person in all manner of practical ways. In engaging in this kind of work Christian people can win the respect of outsiders and a hearing for the gospel. Most of all they can bring glory to Christ.

In general, unbelievers these days are deeply suspicious of the church. The kind of work I have been encouraging in this book might be a case for letting your light shine before men so that they see your good works and glorify your Father in heaven (Matt. 5:14-16). In an inhumane world the church is called upon not only to preach but also to adorn the gospel of Christ and draw attention to the fact that faith works. How can that be too much trouble?

It depends if you're any good

My father-in-law died in his own home, as he had wished to do. To the very last day he was tended by people who knew and loved him. As far as anyone could tell, he suffered no pain and there was no struggle or agitation as he slipped away. The doctor who signed the death certificate was genuinely impressed with the standard of care that Charles had received: he had not one single pressure sore.

In the last few weeks of his life, Charles remained in bed; it was wearisome to him to be hoisted onto the commode. So we cleaned him and turned him several times a day. He slept for most of the time. He spoke very little and his speech was indistinct.

The last conversation I had with him, a couple of days before his death, went something like this:

'Shall I sing to you, Charles?'

Charles opened one eye and gave me one of his withering looks.

'So, you are awake. Would you like me to sing to you?'

'It depends how good you are.' He whispered.

And his lips stretched into the hint of a toothless smile. I knew he still had his sense of humour. I laughed. I sang anyway.

My song that morning categorically denied that goodness has anything to do with anything. It is grace that does the business every time: God's grace to me in all the journey of looking after Charles; his patience with me through all my resentment and failure. As I sang, I caught from Charles, like distant bagpipes, the faintest accompanying drone.

Through many dangers, toils and snares
We have already come.
'Twas grace that brought me safe thus far
And grace will lead me home.

OTHER BOOKS OF INTEREST
FROM
CHRISTIAN FOCUS

aren't they Lovely when they're asleep?

Lessons in unsentimental parenting

ann Benton

Aren't they lovely
when they're asleep?

Lessons in unsentimental parenting

Ann Benton

Ann Benton used to run parenting skills classes in local schools. People kept saying "This is great, where do you get this stuff?" She came clean "Actually, it's from the Bible."

This book contains the wisdom distilled from Ann's popular seminars on parenting the next generation. She uses a 'God's eye view' of what we are really like in order to help people who are seeking to be responsible parents in an increasingly child-centred society.

You will learn six key concepts: accept, beware, communicate, discipline, evaluate and fear the Lord. These are applied with understanding and sensitivity.

At last – a parenting book with authority and easy to understand applications! Each short, punchy chapter is rounded off with thought-provoking questions that will make you want to wake them up and try some new ideas!

ISBN 978-1-85792-876-8

Don't they make a Lovely Couple?

Six Important Questions You Need To Face About Your Marriage

John & Ann Benton

Don't They Make a Lovely Couple:

Six important questions you need to face about your marriage

John and Ann Benton

Only half of today's marriages stick - why is that? The social revolution has made marriage fairer and unacceptable behaviour more 'frowned upon' so shouldn't our marriages be healthier and more long lasting?

Why is it that an institution that forms the basis of society is in crisis? And what can we do to improve things?

Here are the six questions to ask yourselves if you are preparing for, or are already part of, a marriage.

1. WHAT? - The nature of your marriage
2. WHO? - The partners in your marriage
3. WHY? - The reasons for your marriage
4. HOW? - The practicalities of your marriage
5. WHEN? - The timing of your marriage
6. WHERE? - The purpose of your marriage

This book won't make you feel guilty and suggest impossible solutions (we've all read THOSE sort of books before!). It'll make you realise what you can do and suggest a plan to implement it.

Is your marriage important? - Show that it is! There are also two helpful appendices:

1. Pre-marriage Studies
2. Why not? - Sexual temptation in the workplace

ISBN 978-1-84550-046-7

JOHN A. HUFFMAN, JR

the family

HOW TO BUILD AN AUTHENTIC, LOVING HOME

you want

The Family you Want

How to Establish an Authentic, Loving Home

John A. Huffman

Whilst we all have a deep longing to be part of an ideal family, imperfect people make imperfect ones – it's a simple fact of life. Should we, as some in our post-modern society suggest, just give up?

If that thought depresses you then take heart and let John Huffman help you to achieve the best family you can. It won't be perfect but it will be better.

'I highly recommend it... His approach is thoughtful, his style clear... this book is authentic.'

Leighton Ford

"here is healing medicine for all who care about the family"
Harold Myra, *Christianity Today*

'An excellent reference book for young people setting out on the adventure of life, for married couples seeking help in dealing with problems or for ministers involved in counselling extended family situations.'

The Free Church of Scotland Monthly Record

John Huffman has counselled many on family life issues and lectured internationally on the subject. He is the senior minister of St Andrews Presbyterian Church in Newport Beach, California

ISBN 978-1-85792-933-1

WOMANHOOD
REVISITED

A FRESH LOOK AT THE ROLE OF WOMEN IN SOCIETY

ANNE GRAHAM

Womanhood Revisited

A Fresh look at the Role of Women in Society

Anne Graham

Why do so many full-time mothers and homemakers feel inferior to career women? Why do women feel they need to be more like men to be seen to be successful?

In her book Anne Graham suggests it is time to revisit the perfection of creation where woman was created for and from man – equal in value yet different in purpose, to live in co-operation and not competition.

'Anne has brought the roles of men and women under severe scrutiny as she examines the Word of God. Society, fashions and technology may change and advance, but God's Word remains relevant. Anne's efforts have been well worthwhile and will be a challenge and encouragement to all who read it.'

Fiona Castle, Author

'Anne traces God's intentions for women through Scripture, outlines the changing expectations of women through the course of history, and thus presents the present-day dilemma for women in its wider context. It is thus refreshing to be affirmed in our equality of value with men in God's sight, yet also in our unique and complementary differences.'

Joyce Gledhill

Anne Graham trained as a doctor but has spent most of her energy as a wife to Jim, a Baptist minister, mother to four children and grandmother to eight. She is a popular speaker on this subject at home and abroad.

ISBN 978-1-85792-685-9

Large Print Edition

COMFORT
in
SORROW

R.M. McCheyne

Comfort in Sorrow

Large Print Edition

Robert Murray McCheyne

We have all needed comfort at some time in our lives. People search for comfort in all sorts of places, from the empty psychobabble of the self-help book to the oblivion of alcoholism.

The only completely satisfying source of comfort is found in the Bible - and, more particularly, knowing Jesus as a friend.

This is shown in the story of the death of Lazarus. Jesus comforted Lazarus' sisters, Mary and Martha, weeping with them, before going on to raise Lazarus back to life after four days in the grave.

Robert Murray McCheyne looks at this wonderful passage, offering us real encouragement and pointing us to the one true source of comfort - Jesus.

'He answers the question any family would ask in time of trouble - 'Why Lord?' - and points for comfort ... not to friends, the Church or even the Scriptures but to the Lord Himself. You'll feel better after reading this book.'

Scottish Baptist Magazine

Robert Murray McCheyne (1813 - 1843), has had a tremendous impact not only on the people of his generation but through his writings ever since. He died in his thirtieth year and in the seventh year of ministry while he was the pastor of St Peter's Free Church. His epitaph describes him as a man who 'was honoured by his Lord to draw many wanderers out of darkness into the path of life'.

ISBN 978-1-85792-012-3

Christian Focus Publications
publishes books for all ages

Our mission statement –

STAYING FAITHFUL
In dependence upon God we seek to help make His infallible
Word, the Bible, relevant. Our aim is to ensure that the Lord
Jesus Christ is presented as the only hope to obtain forgiveness
of sin, live a useful life and look forward to heaven with Him.

REACHING OUT
Christ's last command requires us to reach out to our world
with His gospel. We seek to help fulfil that by publishing books
that point people towards Jesus and help them develop a
Christ-like maturity. We aim to equip all levels of readers for
life, work, ministry and mission.

Books in our adult range are published in three imprints.
Christian Focus contains popular works including bio-
graphies, commentaries, basic doctrine and Christian living.
Our children's books are also published in this imprint.
Mentor focuses on books written at a level suitable for Bible
College and seminary students, pastors, and other serious
readers. The imprint includes commentaries, doctrinal
studies, examination of current issues and church history.
Christian Heritage contains classic writings from the past.

Christian Focus Publications Ltd.
Geanies House, Fearn, Ross-shire,
IV20 1TW, Scotland, United Kingdom
info@christianfocus.com

www.christianfocus.com